Give me your money!

A Straightforward Guide to

Debt Collection

By

Anthony Reeves

Straightforward Publishing
www.straightforwardco.co.uk

This book was first published as "Give Me Your Money! A guide to debt recovery," in February 2004 by Anthony Reeves. It was produced by Central Publishing Ltd.

Second edition published by Straightforward Publishing in 2005
Revised edition published by Straightforward Publishing in 2007.
Third edition published by Straightforward Publishing in 2009.
This edition published by Straightforward Publishing in 2012.

ISBN: 9781847162328

About the author:

Anthony Reeves is a Fellow of the Chartered Institute of Legal Executives.

Other books by Anthony Reeves:

- "See You In Court!"(1999) published by Elliot Right Way Books.
- "The Employment Handbook" (2003) published by Fitzwarren Publishing.
- "The Litigation Handbook" (2006) published by Fitzwarren Publishing
- "Will I See You In Court" (2009) published by Emerald Publishing
- "The Debt Collecting Merry-Go-Round" (2011) published by Emerald Publishing

Acknowledgement:

Many thanks to the Penguin and Buster

GIVE ME YOUR MONEY!
A Straightforward Guide to Debt Collection

Contents:

Introduction

Successful debt collection is all about making an impact. Requests for payment need to stand out from the crowd. It involves more than sending standard letters. This book considers various methods of debt recovery, as well as explaining the legal procedures for pursuing non-payers through the courts.

The key aspect of this new edition is that debt collection is becoming more difficult. Businesses must recognise that it is even more important than ever to ensure that you take all appropriate measures at an early stage to stay on top of your credit management. Otherwise, it will be a bit like a soldier firing at the enemy with a blind fold; some of the shots might hit the target but more through luck than judgment.

There also needs to be awareness of the remedies available to debtors where debt collectors do not follow acceptable practice as contained in the new Office of Fair Trading Debt Collection Guidelines and the potential for compensation under the Protection from Harassment Act 1997.

In an effort to attempt to level the playing field between creditors and debtors, and so reduce the difficulties of enforcing judgments, the book proposes some radical reforms to the legal process which would greatly speed up the processes of collecting commercial debts.

As in most areas of life, prevention is better than cure. To reduce the risk of being owed money, it is sensible to take precautions before entering into contracts. A little time spent investigating who you intend doing business with can detect warning signs which indicate whether the customer is likely to be a bad payer. It is very important to investigate the financial background of a business or individual. It is possible to build up a reasonable picture of a potential customer by a few basic checks that do not cost much.

This book explains what steps should be taken to satisfy yourself that the person or business you are dealing with is financially sound and likely to pay your bills. Credit information can sometimes be ambiguous and so guidance is given as to what it could mean. The guidance given is not intended as a comprehensive analysis. It highlights only some of the important factors to be considered when making a credit decision.

When it becomes clear that a customer is delaying payment or is refusing to pay, skill is required to recover the debt. It involves using all the information you have about the debtor and placing yourself in a position of control. This book covers the legal aspects of debt recovery, including the importance of carefully drafted terms and conditions of business. However, legal jargon is kept to a minimum to avoid it reading like a textbook instead of a practical guide.

Every business should have a system for chasing late payments. If your procedure for filtering out potentially bad payers is effective, then it will not usually go beyond reminders. When it becomes clear that the customer is delaying payment or is not going to pay, a certain degree of skill will be required to recover the debt. It involves absorbing all the information you have about the debtor and placing yourself in a position of control. Once you reach this position, then the money should come in with the minimum of effort. "Control" does not mean anything that involves threats of physical violence. It is an intellectual exercise aimed at curtailing the game of excuses for non-payment. To try and cut through the excuses, you might have to engage in conversations that lead the debtor in the direction you want to go or write letters that get straight to the point.

This book considers the different approaches to recovering debts depending on whether you are chasing an individual or a company. When chasing a commercial client you will have to consider whether you want to retain a good business relationship with that organisation. It is therefore vital that there is a close relationship between the sales force and the credit control department. The sales force should be educated to understand that a "sale" is not complete until the money is in the bank. Conversely, credit controllers should also see the need to be more lenient in certain situations for the greater good of the company.

Once you have tried all the various telephone and written techniques to recover the money, then court action is an option unless you decide that the debt is not worth pursuing. Recovering a debt through the county court process can be frustrating, but to improve your chances of succeeding it is important to have a good understanding of the legal procedures.

There are strong economic arguments for companies handling small claims in-house. However, with the small claims limit currently at £5,000 (although expected to go up to £10,000) a debt just under this level can represent a considerable sum to a small business. Therefore, it might be worth instructing solicitors to avoid mistakes even though only limited fixed costs can be recovered in the small claims procedure. With court fees increasing on a regular basis, it is important to get the legal paperwork correct.

The Tribunals, Courts and Enforcement Act 2007 has provisions that if implemented could make important changes to enforcement procedures. As mentioned above, the impetus is very much behind helping those who owe money and some provisions that assist debtors, such as debt relief orders have been introduced before the provisions designed to improve the enforcement of debts. The changes under this Act are being gradually introduced. "Gradually" is probably an understatement. Those in the debt collection industry are frustrated that some key aspects as far as debt collection is concerned have been pushed into the long grass. The intention to extend powers to bailiffs was postponed following pressure from various interest groups.

The severe economic downturn in the UK economy since 2008 caused some major high street names to go into Administration and ultimately go under. Most companies will have gone down because of the economic climate and did all they could to pay their liabilities, but there is a genuine suspicion that in some situations rogue directors are taking advantage of insolvency laws that are in urgent need of reform. Such reforms are needed to allow creditors to easily pursue wrong doing by rogue directors who hide behind limited liability and use procedures such as "pre-pack" administrations as a way of dumping debts.

The techniques for debt recovery set out in this book are based on many years experience. However, it is not advisable to sit back on that experience. All good debt collectors need to take account of the changing legislation and practices. The civil court rules have new protocols in respect of pre-court action conduct with requirements as to the information that must be provided by businesses to consumer debtors.

It is not suggested that the techniques in this book will work in every situation. They are merely methods which the author has found to be successful. There will of course be cases where whatever you do the debt will not be paid. However, by giving due consideration to being paid by customers and implementing proper procedures, the chances of being saddled with bad debts should diminish and cash flow should improve.

The law and court procedures described in this book cover claims that come within the jurisdiction of England and Wales. There are separate legal systems in Scotland and Northern Ireland. Therefore, this book does not cover claims that come within the jurisdiction of Scotland or Northern Ireland.

Whilst every effort has been made to ensure that this book provides accurate and expert guidance, it is impossible to predict every situation that may arise. Therefore, the author, publisher and retailer cannot be held liable for any loss or damage caused by the information or any mistakes contained in this book.

Anthony Reeves
June 2012

****

Chapter 1

Credit Checking and Terms of Business

Checking your customers

If a stranger approaches you in the street asking for a loan, would you lend him any money? Put like this, you would probably say no. So why would a business give credit to a new customer whom they know little about? The reason is usually the desire of the sales team to make their figures look healthy. This is understandable as the argument could be that if your company is not prepared to do business, then there is likely to be another one that will. From a credit management view, customers that pay very late or not at all are not worth having as customers because poor cash flow is the death of many small businesses. It is much better to take sensible precautions before entering into a sizeable contract and find out sufficient information about the potential customer, so you can decide if there is a good prospect of being paid. If the financial position of the customer is not as good as you hoped, but you still want to trade with them, then payment terms can be adjusted to reflect this.

The changed economic climate in recent years, as well as the ease with which it is possible to avoid payment because of ineffective court procedures and insolvency laws, should mean that business should take a very simple approach to a poor credit risk; cash on delivery or no delivery!

When taking on a new customer, ensure that sufficient information is obtained about the company or individual. Check the legal status of the organisation. Is it a limited company or a sole trader? If it is a limited company, what is the company registration number and registered office? It may seem obvious to know who you are trading with, but its importance becomes more apparent should your bill remain unpaid and you consider taking legal action. You don't want to waste time and legal fees on suing the wrong company or describing the debtor incorrectly in legal terms.

Sales staff may feel uneasy about asking searching questions when they are trying to close a deal, but this can be overcome by well designed customer application forms and teaching your staff about the relevance of such information. The sales team should obtain the necessary information and then supply it to the credit control team to run the financial checks. With credit reports available instantly online, these checks should take only a few minutes and so the sales team can be given a decision very quickly. Once the credit report is received, the terms and conditions of business should be sent out to the customer for signing by a manager or director. It is important to get the customer to sign their agreement to the terms and conditions of business before you supply goods or services. Tying up these contractual matters at an early stage is important, otherwise technical arguments may arise about whose terms of business prevail and whether in law any enforceable contract came into existence.

At the time of negotiating with a new customer, the basic information required to enable a credit check to be done includes:

- Full Business Name
- Is the business incorporated? If yes, what is the company registration number?
- What is the registered office

- If the business is not incorporated, who is the proprietor of the business?
- What is the home address of the proprietor?
- Tel Number /Fax Number/E-mail
- Trading address if different to that above
- Address where invoices are to be sent

There are various types of credit reports. The more information you require then the more you can expect to pay. You will need to decide how much detail you require. There is a danger of obtaining too much or too little information. Obtain too much information and you might be confused. Too little information and the credit rating might be ambiguous. If you are going to be requiring regular credit checks, it would be sensible to consult a credit checking agency and explain the information you require and to see if they can tailor a report to your requirements.

Certain information on the credit check may highlight a problem with a potential new customer. Among these are the following

- A poor credit score, for example a score of less than 40 out of 100 may indicate a poor payer
- A large number of unsatisfied County Court Judgments
- A company with a low net worth or negative net worth
- The company making losses over a number of years.

The credit report for Joe Bloggs Publishing Limited is not very favourable for a number of reasons; the credit score is very low, there is a large pre-tax loss, a minus net asset figure and recent unsatisfied county court judgments. It could be argued that Joe Bloggs has merely had a bad year in 2006, compared to 2005 and 2004.

A credit report usually gives a credit score. This is often a score out of a hundred based on analysed accounts; the lower the score, the lower the credit rating. A score of 0-20 usually indicates that you should be extremely cautious when trading with that business, as they could be a bad credit risk. Scores of over 50 would indicate that the business is financially sound and should be a good credit risk.

(Figure 1)

Basic Credit Report on: Joe Bloggs Publishing Limited
Date Incorporated: 24 February 1999
Reg. Number: 0000000

Summary:

Date of lat accounts; 1 October 2003

Sales:	*£800,000*
Pre Tax Profit/ (loss)	*£(100,000)*
Working Capital	*£(150,000)*
Net Assets	*£ (8,688)*

Credit Score: 10 Adverse Trading Information

The company has reported a marked trading loss in conjunction with a deficit in shareholders funds. In view of the foregoing, it is suggested that interested parties should not proceed with unsecured dealings without first obtaining a director's guarantee. The risk index allocated to JOE BLOGGS PUBLISHING LIMITED is based on an analysis of the findings recorded above. In view of the very serious nature of this information, the company has been relegated to the highest risk category.

Public Record Information:

County Court Judgements

Period:	*Last 12months*	*13-24 months*	*25-72months*
Number:	*2*		
Value	*£25,000*		

Profit & Loss

Year ending	**Oct 06**	**Oct 05**	**Oct 04**
Turnover	*800,000*	*700,000*	*645,000*
Profit/ (loss)	*(100,000)*	*30,000*	*46,000*

A company with a long list of unsatisfied county court judgments against its name usually indicates a poor payer. It is not uncommon for large companies to have several judgments against its name, especially where they have many branches. It may be that the various branches are not very well co-ordinated or the organisation will pay in its own time and is not bothered if it incurs a few court judgments along the way. Such large organisations may not be bothered by the effect of county court judgments on their credit rating because their net worth is so large. However, if you trade with them, you might expect them to be particularly slow at paying but you should eventually see your money. It is likely that where county court judgments had been obtained against these large businesses, they would probably have received their money if the creditor had pressed to enforce the judgment.

If the company is small or is a sole trader and the net worth of the business is low, it would be advisable not to trade with them if there are unsatisfied county court judgments. They will probably have other creditors already trying to obtain payment of their judgment and so it might be trying to juggle payments. With a low net worth, they may be on the verge of insolvency and unless you have your debt secured, then you may be behind a long list of others creditors in the liquidation.

Of course it might be that a company with several county court judgments or a poor credit score is simply going through a bad period and that as the business cycle picks up, they will return to their former financial strength. This could be the case where a business has been established for many years. If it has been trading for a long time, then the chances are it will get through its current difficulties. On the other hand, there may be fundamental problems with the business and you should be cautious about trading with it.

As with most statistics, they should be read with a word of warning. The information can be ambiguous. Although the credit score can present a poor picture of a particular business, such reports can be open to various interpretations.

Trade and Bank References

If any of the main indicators on a credit report shows a potential problem with the customer, then you may wish to request trade or bank references. These may be of some help in getting a feel of the customer's payment history, but remember that another customer is unlikely to give definite statements about a trading partner for fear of upsetting a client or running the risk of legal action for a negligent statement. A bank reference is also likely to be couched in cautious language.

Register of Court Judgments

This is maintained by Registry Trust Ltd in London on behalf of the Court Service. The Register of County Court Judgments was recently extended to include High Court Judgments for judgments on or after the 6th April 2006 and Fines in default registered by local justice centres. The register is now known as "The Register of Judgments, Orders and Fines (for England & Wales)". You can search the register to see if there are judgments registered against an individual or business over the previous 6 years, together with the fee of £8.00.

Personal Guarantees

If there are doubts about the credit worthiness of a company or if the company has only recently been incorporated and there are no filed accounts to analyse, it is worth considering obtaining a personal guarantee from a director of the company. Some companies may not take kindly to such a request, but if they refuse then it may be the factor which makes you decide not to trade with the company. On the other hand, some would argue that limited liability is there to protect the directors from personal liability if the company fails. I have also heard clients say that asking for a personal guarantee from the director is something that would simply push them to do business with their competitor. That may be the case but if a potential new customer take offence at being asked for such a personal guarantee then maybe that prospective customer is giving you warning signs that they may be a problem payer in the future. A sample personal guarantee is as set out below, but you should always seek legal advice on the document to ensure it is suited to the particular transaction you are wanting to guarantee.

Sample Guarantee Agreement

The sample director's personal guarantee overleaf concerns David Smith, director of D Smith Ltd, guaranteeing payment for goods and services supplied to D Smith Ltd by Reeves Ltd.

See overleaf.

PERSONAL GUARANTEE

Reeves Ltd 13 Bolton Road Newtown NW10 4RT	D Smith Ltd 10 Market Place Newtown NW4 5YH	David Smith The Manor House Leafy Crescent Newtown NW14 5LP
Herein after referred to as the 'supplier'	Herein after referred to as 'the customer'	Herein after referred to as 'the guarantor'

1. In consideration of the supplier supplying goods and/or services to the Customer, the Guarantor agrees to guarantee payment of all due amounts invoiced to the customer as at today's date.

2. The supplier can enforce this guarantee at anytime on default of one payment. The Guarantors liability will not be affected by the Supplier affording the Customer time to pay on default or initiating any arrangement to rectify any default.

3. The supplier can cancel this guarantee at any time by writing to the Guarantor and/or Customer.

4. The Guarantor and Customer can cancel this guarantee at any time by writing to the supplier at the above address. The guarantee will cover all transactions up to the acknowledgement of the cancellation by the supplier.

A deed is a document that has to be signed and witnessed and the document itself should state that it is executed and delivered as a deed. Normally, for an agreement to be binding there has to be consideration. The above sample guarantee contains consideration, but where there is no consideration the document should be signed as a deed.

The nature of your business

At the end of the day, you have to decide whether or not to deal with a particular customer. In certain sectors of the economy, it would not be practical to make more than sensible checks on a new customer. In some areas of business, such as employment agencies, the customer usually requires the service to be supplied quite quickly. The employment agency which supplies temporary staff is involved in a very competitive market. Production companies that need packers and other staff at short notice may decide to try another agency if you delay too long in offering a quote. It will require your credit control staff to make checks very quickly to avoid the loss of business. Recruitment consultants (who are effectively sales staff) will often be under pressure to send temporary workers to new customers before credit checks have been undertaken. If they supply staff before doing credit checks, the employment agency is taking a risk because they usually pay the workers at the end of the week they worked, which could be a long time before they actually get paid by the client. The employment agency could be carrying this expense for 90 days. It should consider whether the potential new customer, if in financial difficulty, could be using an employment agency to avoid a large wage bill.

The extent of the credit checks you undertake will depend on the type and size of your business. It is unlikely a small firm will go through a large credit checking process on every single account. It will be a case of undertaking checks that are proportionate to the size of the contract which you are entering into. For example, a small building firm that is about to sign a contract for a substantial project should take greater care to check out who it is doing business with, as default by the other party would seriously jeopardise its future existence. A small contract may not make or break a firm if there was default on payment. When the economy is experiencing a general downturn, there are competing theories as to whether or not a company should do business with companies that find it difficult to meet your strict payment terms. Certain customers that may have previously had a respectable credit rating may show a potential payment problem.

Terms of Business

All businesses, other than those engaged in the most straightforward of transactions, should have a document which sets out the standard terms on which it does business. The importance of having an understandable contract should not be forgotten when it comes to credit control. The terms should be unambiguous because if there is uncertainty over the terms of the contract, it will usually be interpreted against the person seeking to rely on the unclear clause. It is also vital to ensure that the terms form part of any resulting contract.

The general position in law is that the customer should have notice of the terms of business when the contract is formed. A problem that can arise is that the parties may fax over the front side of a double sided document and unless the terms are seen by the other party, it will usually be the case that those terms will not apply. However, a recent Court of Appeal decision in ***Rooney v CSE Bournemouth [2010]***means that there can be situations where terms are incorporated into a contract which may have not been seen. In this case, the defendant (CSE) sought to rely on its standard terms and conditions which, it argued, had been incorporated by reference into a contract because the words "terms and conditions available on request" were written at the bottom of a work order form, which the claimant (Rooney) had signed. The Court of Appeal held that these words were, in principle, capable of being understood as an intention to incorporate a party's standard terms and conditions into a contract. Lord Justice Toulson indicated that this was the most likely interpretation of the wording and considered that it would be commercially most odd to have a contract for the performance of services where commercial terms were left by the contractor to be included at the customer's request.

It should be remembered that the decision in ***Rooney v CSE Bournemouth*** was only in respect of an appeal concerning an application to strike out part of the defence and not a full hearing. The message that should be conveyed to all staff is to ensure they bring the terms of the contract to the attention of the other party before the agreement is completed.

When dealing with a company, especially a new company or one that does not have a good credit history, it would be advisable to get a director of the company to sign an order form which confirms that the director believes the company is able to pay for the goods. The significance of this is explained later in Chapter 7 when the case of ***Contex Drouzhba Ltd v. Wiseman (2007)*** is considered.

It is often the case that each party to a proposed agreement tries to insist that its standard terms apply. The general position is that the last party to put forward its terms before the agreement will have their terms forming the contract. However, it may depend on the particular circumstances of a case.

Whether or not a company accepted the terms of business absolutely, has caused legal cases over whose terms and conditions prevail. This has become known as "the battle of the forms". The acceptance of terms is important to credit control and so it is worth considering the legal position. The leading case in this area is ***Butler v. Ex-Cell-O Corporation (England) Ltd [1979]***. The principle from this case is that an acceptance which does not accept all the terms of the original offer is not a true acceptance but a counter-offer which "kills off" the original offer and amounts to a new offer which can be accepted.

The decision in the case of *Butler* is the traditional approach of the courts. It is said to provide a degree of certainty. It has been criticised for being too rigid and can place the party in receipt of the last communication in a difficult situation. The following example explains the importance it can have in respect to credit control.

Ewan Swan is the senior sales manager with Brampton Employment Agency. He visits a client, Porky Pies Ltd, who asks him to give a quote on the cost of supplying temporary workers to his factory. Ewan gives Porky Pies a quote for the cost of supplying temporary workers. At the same time, he gives them a copy of Brampton's standard terms of business. One of the standard terms is that payment is 14 days from the date of invoice. Porky Pies think about the quote. A week later, Ewan's junior assistant (Lee Gamble) receives an order form from Porky Pies requesting 10 temporary factory packers. The form states that this order is placed subject to Porky Pies standard terms of business which are printed on the back. One of the terms states that Porky Pies pays 90 days from the date of invoice.

If Brampton's supply the temps, then it is likely that the terms of Porky Pies will have been accepted with the less favourable payment terms which causes a potential problem for credit control. The reasoning is that Ewan made an offer in the quote and the accompanying terms and conditions. Porky Pies make a counter offer on their terms. If temporary workers are then supplied, then the contract is likely to have been concluded on Porky Pies terms and conditions.

To avoid the chances of this happening, Ewan should ensure that he obtains a signed acceptance of Brampton's terms and conditions before workers are supplied.

Terms relating to payment

To improve the chances of being paid on time, it is important to have clear terms relating to charges and the date on which they become due. In view of the recent difficult economic times as well as the costs and lack of effectiveness of court enforcement processes, there is a very strong argument to require new customers to provide money on account and make greater use of putting accounts on stop if payments slip too far behind. Some businesses might say that this not the way they like to do business as they like to have good customer relations but the current times require a touch of realism to ensure you are not holding a bag of bad debts.

Where you are providing services, it would be prudent to consider provisions within the contract to permit staged payments. Without such a provision, there may be problems involving arguments about whether or not there has been substantial performance. In the case of ***Bolton v. Mahadeva (1972),*** the claimant agreed with the defendant that he would install central heating in the defendant's house for a lump sum of £560. When the work was completed, the defendant complained that it was defective and refused to pay. The Judge found that the flue was defective and that the system was inefficient in that the amount of heat varied from room to room. The cost of rectifying the defects was £174. The Court of Appeal held that the claimant was not entitled to recover as there had not been substantial performance.

The point of this case is that unless you completed performance or substantially completed performance, then you may not recover until the job has been done unless you have provisions in the contract permitting staged payments.

Payment

All payments required to be made pursuant to this Agreement by either party shall be made within 14 days of the date of the relevant invoice without any set-off, withholding or deduction except such amount (if any) of tax as that party is required to deduct or withhold by law.

A set-off is where a defendant asserts a counterclaim against the claimant based on an event or transaction other than the event or transaction that forms the basis of the claimant's claim. It has the particular aim of defeating or diminishing the amount the defendant will have to pay the claimant. What often happens in debt collection is that the debtor will say that the creditor owes the debtor money and so attempts to deduct this from the amount on the invoice. Having a clause which says "without any set-off, withholding or deduction" means that the debtor should pay the invoice without deducting any amount in respect of any claim he alleges he may have against the creditor. If the debtor is determined to pursue a claim, then he must first pay the invoice in full and then pursue any claim he may have. This type of clause may encounter problems where the customer is a consumer, as it may be regarded as an unfair contract term but is unlikely to be construed in this way if it is commercial customer.

Interest for Late Payment

Many terms and conditions of business have clauses which charge interest on late payment. Under the Late Payment of Commercial Debts (Interest) Act 1998 as amended by the EU Directive which was implemented on 7 August 2002, all businesses may charge interest and fixed compensation for late payment. Even if the terms of business do not refer to the legislation, its provisions are implied into the contract. However, it is better to have a clause in your terms of business. The provisions of the legislation only apply where the customer is acting in the course of business, so would not apply against a consumer. The Late Payment legislation permits interest to be charged at the rate of 8% above the base rate on accounts after 30 days from the date of the invoice or when the goods were delivered or services provided. If different payment terms have been agreed, then interest can be charged when payment becomes due under the contract. The level of compensation which may be charged for late payment in addition to interest depends on the amount of the debt:

- For debts below £1,000: £40 in compensation
- For debts from £1,000 to £10,000: £70 in compensation
- For debts over £10,000: £100 in compensation

These fixed charges were introduced to help compensate creditors for the costs of chasing late payment.

The creditor is required to warn the debtor that late payment charges will be claimed unless payment is received by a specified date. If the debtor does not pay the interest and compensation then ultimately you will have to take court action. If the debtor has paid the principal sum but not the late payment charges, then it may not always be deemed economic to pursue these costs. A debtor can argue against paying late charges if it can be shown that the delay in payment was caused by the creditor or that they decided that it is unreasonable to award the late payment charges in all the circumstances.

Retention of Title

Every supplier of goods should include retention of title clauses in their contract terms unless they always obtain payment before delivery. Retention of title clauses allow a supplier to retain ownership over the goods supplied until the buyer has made payment, thus providing the supplier with a form of security against the buyer's failure to pay or insolvency. This clause states that the buyer does not obtain ownership of the goods unless and until payment is made. Such a clause can and should go further and include what is called "an all monies clause", which retains ownership until all monies due to the supplier have been paid by the buyer. If the buyer goes out of business before paying for the goods the supplier can retrieve them. It is often not as simple as that but such clauses certainly can work and are used on a regular basis against liquidators with great effect. The following is an example of a retention title clause, but it is obviously advisable to seek advice on the particular circumstances where you want such a clause in your terms and conditions.

Retention of Title Clause

1. *The legal and beneficial title of the Goods shall not pass to the Buyer until the Supplier has received in cash or cleared funds payment in full of the price of the Goods and any other goods supplied by the Supplier and the Buyer has repaid all moneys owed to the Supplier, regardless of how such indebtedness arose.*
2. *Until payment has been made to the Supplier in accordance with these Conditions and title in the Goods has passed to the Buyer, the Buyer shall be in possession of the Goods as bailee for the Supplier and the Buyer shall store the Goods separately and in an appropriate environment, shall ensure that they are identifiable as being supplied by the Supplier and shall insure the Goods against all reasonable risks.*
3. *The Buyer shall not be entitled to pledge or in any way charge by way of security for any indebtedness any of the goods which remain the property of the Supplier, but if the Buyer does so all money owing by the Buyer to the Supplier shall (without prejudice to any other right or remedy of the Supplier) forthwith become due and payable.*

4. *The Supplier reserves the right to repossess any Goods in which the Supplier retains title without notice. The Buyer irrevocably authorises the Supplier to enter the Buyer's premises during normal business hours for the purpose of repossessing the Goods in which the Supplier retains title and inspecting the Goods to ensure compliance with the storage and identification requirements*
5. *The Buyer's right to possession of the Goods in which the Supplier maintains legal and beneficial title shall terminate if;*
    - *i.* *The Buyer commits or permits any material breach of his obligations under these Conditions;*
    - *ii.* *The Buyer enters into a voluntary arrangement under Part 1 of the Insolvency Act 1986, or any other scheme or arrangement is made with his creditors;*
    - *iii.* *The Buyer is or becomes the subject of a bankruptcy order or takes advantage of any other statutory provision for the relief of insolvent debtors;*
    - *iv.* *The Buyer convenes any meeting of its creditors, enters into voluntary or compulsory liquidation, has a receiver, manager, administrator or administrative receiver appointed in respect of its assets or undertaking or any part thereof, any documents are filed with the court for the appointment of an administrator in respect of the Buyer, notice of intention to appoint an administrator is given by the Buyer or any of its directors or by a qualifying floating charge-holder, a resolution is passed or petition presented to any court for the winding up of the*

Buyer or for the granting of an administration order in respect of the Buyer, or any proceedings are commenced relating to the insolvency or possible insolvency of the Buyer.

Most liquidators will usually argue that the retention of title clauses is invalid. This is not surprising as they have a vested interest in defeating all retention of title claims, simply because there will be more assets to realise when proceedings are concluded so that secured creditors/debenture holders can be paid.

Enforcing retention of title clauses can be a battle of wills. Before deciding what to do, you should seek legal advice to confirm what the position is in your particular case. To seek to enforce retention of title clauses when a company is in Administration will either require the permission of the Administrator or the Court.

Early notification of queries

Another important clause to have in your terms and conditions is one that requires the buyer to inform the supplier of any queries soon after the delivery of the goods or services. This clause stops the customer from inventing queries or complaints as an excuse for non-payment. It also gives you an immediate opportunity to resolve any problem to the customer's satisfaction, thereby reducing the possibility of the customer requesting a refund.

A sample clause is as follows:

'Queries and/or complaints must be notified to the supplier verbally or in writing within seven (7) days of receipt of the goods (service) and/or invoice, whichever is the latter.'

The relationship between credit control and other parts of a company

In some companies, the sales department views credit control as an irritation. They regard the caution displayed by credit controllers as excessive and feel restricted in their opportunity to earn bonuses through commission. To avoid these attitudes, it is vital to have good communication between the credit control department and its sales force, and indeed all sections of the organisation. It is important that all relevant staff should be made aware of the company's policy in respect of credit. This may alleviate the "them and us" attitude and hopefully install the belief that it is in everyone's interest to ensure that customers pay on time. In many cases, it is a matter of maintaining a good relationship with the sales force.

Where there is good communication, the salesman will provide the information needed by credit control to judge a potential new customer. Obviously there will be some sales staff that are only interested in closing a deal and will not confer with credit control. In such situations, the credit controller has to inform the appropriate manager or director of what is happening before a spate of bad debts appear on the ledger. To avoid this, sales staff could be penalised by having their commission reduced if an unpaid account which has to be written off was acquired without the sales person going through the approved credit checking procedure. This may seem harsh but it supports the important philosophy that a sale is not complete until the money is in the bank.

Maintaining relationships with the sales staff and having policies which penalise bonuses are not always easy to implement. In some types of industries, the sales staff are very much "here today gone tomorrow". In sectors such as the recruitment industry, the turnover of sales staff (or "consultants" as they are called) is very high. In these industries as in others, the sales staff may primarily be concerned with making a high level of commission and have little regard for the impact on the credit management of the company.

The Layout of Invoices

Having supplied goods or services a company will usually produce an invoice to send out to the customer to obtain payment. It is vital for credit control that the layout of the invoice is correct. Some of the points to consider when setting out an invoice may seem obvious but it is surprising how many firms pay little attention to the wording of such an important document. Your customers may take advantage of poorly drafted invoices. An invoice should:

- State the amount due
- State the person or organisation that is responsible for paying the amount due on the invoice
- State the name of any contact within the company where the invoice is to be sent
- A brief but sufficient description of what the invoice relates to, quoting any reference where appropriate
- A statement of the payment terms and the date by which payment should arrive

An example of the way to lay out an invoice is set out below in Figure 2.

(See overleaf).

(Figure 2.)

Reeves Publishing Ltd
20 Market Street, Upton, UP1 3NH
Tel. 0100 01111 VAT No. X11222

INVOICE

To: *Joe Bloggs Ltd, 10 Market Place, Upmarket, UP1 3NH*

Invoice Number: *001* ***Date:*** *1 October 2006*
Purchase Order Number/Your ref: *00001*

Details:
The production of 5,000 hardback books as ordered under the contract dated 1 August 2006.

Amount Due: £10,000

Please ensure that we receive payment by: *21 October 2006*
Cheques should be made payable to: *"Reeves Publishing Ltd"*
Your Payment should be sent to:
20 Market Street, Upton, UP1 3NH

BACS payments should be made to the following bank account:
Upton Bank Ltd, Sort Code: 01-02-00 Account Number: 0100000

Chapter 2

Chasing Commercial Debts

This chapter considers the various situations that could be faced when chasing commercial debts. Although the circumstances of one outstanding debt are unlikely to be identical to another, it is possible after years of experience to identify the reasons and excuses for non payment. Effective debt recovery is about being alert to warning signs which you are aware of from previous experience. This may mean you are perceived as dealing with a client without an open mind, but your aim as a debt collector is to recover money which will maintain your company's cash flow.

Some of the common categories of non-payer include:

- "There is nobody around to sign cheques"
- "We are a big company and will pay when we are ready"
- "We will pay you when we get paid by our customers"
- "The company is facing financial difficulties and is trying to resolve these difficulties, but if you keep pressing us then you will end up with nothing"
- "We ignore all requests for payment and only make payment when things have gone right to the wire, i.e. when court action is literally being prepared."

It is amazing how many large companies enter freely into contracts knowing the payment terms and yet they rarely seem to honour them. A small supplier may be so pleased at having achieved a deal with a major company that it feels reluctant to rock the boat when payment stretches beyond the agreed time period. The small company feels that the big client may take its business elsewhere if it gets tough over payment. Undoubtedly that happens but experience suggests that companies with whom you have to get tough come back to do more business or continue trading with you, because large companies regard such matters as "just business". Directors of large companies don't take such matters personally. It is part of a day's work that they push matters as far as they can go. Maybe that is how the large company grew by not giving way too easily. Similarly, if the smaller company takes a stance it would signify that it is determined to get on in the market place and not be taken for a ride. After all, a large part of being successful in business is being prepared to take calculated risks.

It has been argued that companies, with whom you have had to get tough with, do return to trade with you. If a large company ceases trading on acrimonious terms, but is a bad payer by nature, it may find it difficult to obtain another supplier who will tolerate late payment. In which case, they often return wanting to start afresh. In such a case, the small company can take advantage and negotiate from a position of strength.

VL Transport Plc

VL Transport Plc is a large transport company that specialises in distributing white goods. For the past 4 years, VL has used agency drivers from Marsh Employment Agency. The contract with VL was acquired soon after Marsh began and although the standard payment terms of Marsh have always been 21 days from the date of invoice, no written agreement was actually signed. Being a new agency, they were pleased with having obtained a large customer and over the years, payment often took 90 days to arrive. However, Marsh has now reached a situation where they seriously need to improve their cash flow.

The credit controller for Marsh, Mrs Receiver, regularly telephones the purchase ledger department at VL. Over recent years, the calls chasing payment by Mrs Receiver have followed similar patterns. Shortly after the invoice became due, she would speak to Sharon in the purchase ledger section of VL Transport.

A typical conversation between Sharon and Mrs Receiver was:

"Hello Sharon, how are you?"

"Fine Mary."

"Just checking Sharon that you have us on the payment run for this Friday."

"Far as I can see, you should be on the next run."

"Thanks Sharon, look forward to receiving payment."

This short conversation between Sharon and Mrs Receiver indicates already that Mrs Receiver is not in control. A better approach is discussed later.

10 days after the date when Mrs Receiver was expecting to have received payment of the invoice, she decides to give Sharon another call.

"Hello Sharon, Mrs Receiver from Marsh Employment Agency here. I thought you said we would be on the payment run for last Friday."

"I think you misunderstood me. The next payment run is not until the end of the month. Anyhow, I'll try and get you on the next payment run."

As it is 2 weeks until the end of the month, payment of the invoice is going to be at least 4 weeks late. A few days before the end of the month, Mrs Receiver receives a further call from Sharon at VL Transport.

"Hi Mary, I'm not going to get you the cheque on Friday. All the directors are out of the office and so we can't get cheques signed. Also, one of the invoices, (no. 12345) is under query. The invoice does not have a purchase order number on it. Can you let me have the order number? We can't pay without a purchase order number."

Mrs Receiver obtains the purchase order number from the driving controller and sends it to Sharon. This takes up another week before she is able to reply to Sharon with the purchase order number. She is told that that all the invoices (totalling £4,500) will be paid on the cheque run at the end of the week. Payment of the invoices is now some 6 weeks late. The credit terms were 21 days from the date of the invoice. It is now heading towards 75 days from the date of the bill. However, this is not the end of the sequence of excuses. Mrs Receiver rings Sharon the day before the payment run to confirm that payment will be made. Sharon is not available as she is on holiday and is put through to a colleague in purchase ledger accounts. Mrs Receiver is told that there will not be payment for another 10 days as the Finance Director is on holiday and so there is no one to sign the cheques. VL Transport has managed to extend the credit period up to 90 days from the date of the invoice. Mrs Receiver is exasperated! What should she do to avoid this situation?

There are number of ways in which Mrs Receiver could assert more control over Sharon. In the first conversation, Mrs Receiver should have obtained a precise date and amount of the payment. "The next cheque run" is too vague. Sharon could argue that she only said "should be on the next cheque run" and did not actually specify the date of the cheque run. Sharon exploits this point in the next conversation. During the second conversation, Mrs Receiver should have obtained a firm commitment as to the next cheque run. It would have also have been a good time to raise the question of charging interest for late payment if VL Transport do not adhere to this commitment. In addition, Mrs Receiver should send a short follow up e-mail/fax confirming what was said. This might read as follows:

To: Sharon@vltransport.co.uk
From: areceiver@marsh.co.uk
Subject: Your Overdue Account Date: 15 October

Sharon,
Just to confirm our conversation today, in which you stated that we would be receiving £4,500 on the 29 October. I mentioned that should you not make this payment as promised, we reserve the right to charge interest for late payment under the Late Payment of Commercial Debts (Interest) Act 1998, as amended and supplemented by the Late Payment of Commercial Debt Regulations 2002.

The purpose of mentioning the Late Payment legislation is twofold. It increases the pressure on the debtor but before charging late payment interest, you have to tell the debtor of your intention to use this legislation.

When Sharon speaks to Mrs Receiver for the third time, saying payment will not be made for reasons of no signed cheques and purchase order numbers, alarm bells should be sounding at Marsh Employment. It is vital that Mrs Receiver takes control on this occasion. She needs to point out the irrelevance of the need for purchase order numbers, especially as Sharon stated in a previous conversation that payment would be made without any mention of purchase order numbers. In any case, there has been no dispute that Marsh Employment has supplied the workers and so payment is due. As to the excuse of not having a director to sign cheques, Mrs Receiver could make the point that VL Transport's internal administration is not her concern as they have had plenty of time to sort out their cheque signing arrangements. At this point, Mrs Receiver would be well advised to send the following letter to the Finance Manager, Mr Payer:

2 November

Dear Mr Payer,

FINAL DEMAND

I refer to the conversation with Sharon and was disappointed that you have failed to meet your promise to pay by the 29 October as agreed in our conversation on 15 October. We have not received any valid reason for non payment. I should make it clear that we cannot allow accounts to remain unpaid.

This account is considerably overdue and ***unless we receive payment of £4,500 by 9 November,*** *then we will pass the matter to our legal section to issue county court proceedings to recover the amount outstanding. Interest and compensation will also be charged according to the Late Payment of Commercial Debts (Interest) Act 1998 as amended and supplemented by the Late Payment of Commercial Debt Regulations 2002. In addition, a stop will be put on your account preventing any further temporary drivers being supplied until the amount is cleared.*

Yours sincerely

Marsh Employment

Drivel & Co. Limited

Smith & Jones Employment Agency supply temporary warehouse workers to Drivel and Co Ltd. Drivel signed an agreement with Smith & Jones two years ago with the terms being that payment of Smith & Jones' invoice would be within 21 days of the invoice date. For the first 6 months that they traded together, Drivel paid the invoices about 4 weeks late, which meant that they had nearly 50 days credit. The account had an average turnover of around £1,000 per month, and when Drivel were pressed for payment they would first of all say that the cheque is out for signature with the Finance Director. After a bit more persuasion the cheque usually arrives. They always paid but it was late and required much pressure from the credit controller. After 6 months, Drivel's payment record became worse and the average time it took to receive payment rose to 90 days. When Smith & Jones' pressed for payment they would have no luck in speaking to a Director. Eventually, court action was threatened and a substantial payment was received. Drivel was a bit annoyed but the two companies continued trading. Again the account became well overdue and invoices dating back nearly 90 days were still outstanding. This time, Smith & Jones were starting to get very concerned as the account had built up to £4,500 and Drivel were informed that unless payment was made within 7 days, county court action would start. The Managing Director of Drivel then made contact stating that he was very annoyed with the approach of Smith & Jones and said that 90 days was what he paid on and not would budge. If Smith & Jones did not like it then he would take his business elsewhere.

Having too many customers that extend the credit terms can be damaging to cash flow. Whether a company can sustain regular late payers may depend on the type of market in which it does business. Smith and Jones is an employment agency that deals in the supply of temporary workers. They supply temporary office staff such as secretaries and receptionists, temporary warehouse staff and temporary drivers. It is a fast flowing market place with temporary workers entering the agency's books one week and then leaving them another. These temporary workers are paid at the end of each week and so the agency is carrying a large financial burden. Their clients do not have to meet NI contributions and PAYE. It is vital that an employment agency's customer pays on time so that they have the cash flow to cover the large weekly wage bill of the temporary workers.

In deciding whether to continue trading with Drivel & Co, Smith & Jones should try and decide the customer's real intentions. Is this a last ditch attempt to avoid insolvency? If this is the case, then there is a danger that Drivel & Co. will not be too concerned about paying Smith & Jones. If Drivel & Co is fighting a battle to survive, they could be using an employment agency to avoid having to pay a large wages bill. Smith & Jones would be advised to proceed quickly and recover the money due to them. Waiting until 90 days would not be prudent. A trade debt to an employment agency is not a secured debt and so if Drivel & Co becomes insolvent they would probably receive very little if anything at all if the company was wound up. Applying pressure at an early stage may produce some payment. The company may pay the most vocal creditors, while it attempts to struggle on or hide the real picture for as long as possible. This may end up being more than the meagre amount paid out on insolvency. Unfortunately, the only people who seem to benefit from insolvency are the liquidators, who charge what many would regard as excessive fees. The report from the liquidator often shows that the value of realised assets is only a little more than the liquidator's fee, leaving a small amount to be distributed to creditors.

Some businesses in the situation of Drivel & Co. may not have any financial problems but still decide to take advantage of Smith &

Jones by refusing to pay within the agreed time and delaying payment to suit themselves. How can you tell if this is what a customer is doing? A large company may fall into this category. They may take the attitude that the company has a certain amount of market power and that it can keep its suppliers waiting until it is ready to pay. They might also think that some of its smaller suppliers would not have the nerve to contemplate legal action. If a small supplier did take the initiative and start county court action, they will either pay up at this point or delay further by hoping that the small supplier will be too daunted by the might of their legal department. These type of late payers are quite prepared to wait until the Court Claim arrives and do not seem to mind incurring the legal costs. What should be remembered by the small supplier is that since the introduction of the Woolf Reforms in April 1999, county court procedure has been simplified and the small claims limit increased, making it easier to pursue a debt through the courts without a solicitor. However, getting a court judgment in a small claim might be easier, but what has become difficult is enforcing the judgment.

Chapter 3

Chasing an Individual Debtor

Recovering a debt from an individual debtor involves different skills and techniques than those used for chasing money from a business. It may be argued that it is more difficult to recover debts from an individual who is hard up or without a fixed address. On the other hand, it may be easier to recover debts from some individuals because it is personal to the debtor and so you are more likely to provoke a response. Having achieved a response, you have an opportunity to negotiate a repayment plan. Small but regular instalments are probably the best you can expect. Even if you go to court and obtain judgment, the debtor can ask the court to order payment by low weekly instalments. Sometimes, a debtor's statement of their financial circumstances shows excessive expenditure on certain items. In such cases, the creditor may wonder whether the debtor is trying to disguise the true extent of their financial position.

Many people end up in financial difficulty by refusing to deal with problems early enough or simply by ignoring reminder letters. It is surprising how many people who are in financial trouble have a pile of unopened letters. It is important not to ignore reminders as many creditors, if approached earlier on would probably accept small regular amounts than spend money on court fees, especially as recent court fees increases has made legal action an expensive process. The "burying the head in the sand" attitude of some debtors makes using the telephone so important. Some people who have not responded to your chasing letters may have literacy problems. If you have a telephone number for the debtor then do not delay in calling them.

The importance of telephone chasing

The telephone can be the most effective tool in debt collection. In many cases, you might only get one chance to speak to a debtor and so it important not to waste the opportunity to make an impact. You should also take full advantage of the opportunity as if you do not make the impact on that one call or possibly in a follow up call, then you have probably lost a realistic chance of getting an early settlement. Some organisations take the view that it does not matter if you do not achieve success in these early conversations as their policies involve a whole string of calls in a short space of time. This could easy lead to a claim of harassment and this is explored later in the chapter.

Some of the key elements of telephone chasing are:

- Listening
- Asking questions which gain information about their circumstances
- Keeping control of the direction of the conversation thus leading to payment commitments
- Where the debtor is clearly not giving you the correct information, explain why you know what you are being told is not correct.
- Close the call by summarizing the discussion and confirming any agreements.

Those engaged in telephone chasing will have undoubtedly come across a debtor who replies with a blunt "I have no money to pay you!" How do you try and get through this apparent stonewall? The debtor probably thinks that this closed response will stop the debt collector in their tracks. The experienced collector should relish this type of reply as they can use all of their skills and it makes telephone chasing an interesting challenge.

To illustrate ways forward in this situation, consider the following dialogue between Gale and Mr Unresponsive. Gale is a housing officer for Salberry Housing Association and Mr Unresponsive is a tenant who wants to transfer to a larger property.

Gale: I am ringing you to discuss payment of the rent arrears on your account. I see that you are in arrears by £300. I need to discuss an arrangement to pay these arrears.
Mr. Unresponsive: I can't afford to pay anything!
Gale: What are your circumstances?
Mr. Unresponsive: What do you mean?
Gale: Are you working at the moment?
Mr. Unresponsive: Why should I tell you! You've not given me an answer about my request for a transfer to a bigger property.
Gale: I need information so we can discuss what you can afford. We will usually not consider a transfer unless there is a clear rent account or there is an arrangement to pay the arrears.
Mr. Unresponsive: Oh I see. I drive vans for Salberry Fruit Supplies. Don't earn much though.
Gale: What is roughly your weekly wage?
Mr. Unresponsive: About £225 per week. But then I've got my bills to pay.
Gale: Yes and rent is a very important bill. How about you pay £10 per week on top of your current rent of £65?
Mr. Unresponsive: Can't afford £10, but I can manage £6 per week.
Gale: I'll agree to that. I would like the first payment with next week's rent. I'll send you a letter confirming this arrangement. Thank you for calling Mr. Unresponsive.

Gale displays a good technique for getting Mr Unresponsive to agree to an arrangement. He initially refuses to discuss payment of the arrears but once Gale explains that she is helping him by seeing what he can afford and stating that it would help his transfer application, Mr Unresponsive becomes less obstructive. It is obviously important that Gale phrases this conversation in the right tone and emphasizes the words "would not usually" when mentioning his transfer request. Otherwise, it may come across as a threat. When negotiating, we want to use levers to persuade people to pay and not make it sound like blackmail. Gale has arrived at the desired result after a relatively short conversation, which illustrates the effectiveness of using the telephone to chase debts. The level of payment, £6 plus the current rent, may not seem much but a court would probably not order any more where the person is on a low income. Now that the arrangement has been made, Gale should quickly send the confirmation letter and monitor the account to check that payments are made as agreed.

When chasing an individual for money, it is important to consider all the information about the person. The example of Bob Giles and RG Accountants illustrates the importance of reviewing the information about the debtor and making use of it.

Bob Giles and RG Accountants

Bob Giles is a farmer who owns Upton Bassett Farm. He employed RG Accountants to prepare his tax return and advise on other aspects of his financial affairs. Bob Giles has used RG Accountants for many years and so knows the partners in the firm fairly well. Bob has failed to settle RG's latest invoice for £3,000 after being outstanding for several months. The partner who conducted the work has sent several chasing letters to which he had no reply. RG Accountants have telephone numbers for Bob Giles, including his mobile number. Sharon, RG's credit controller, is given the file and instructed to collect the debt.

As RG have dealt with Bob's financial affairs, they have plenty of information which if used correctly should greatly improve their chances of recovering the outstanding bill. It may be that Bob has not responded to letters because he has literacy problems. The partner who dealt with his matter should have a good idea as to his difficulties with reading letters. Sharon can see from the file that Bob Giles has written several well structured letters to the partner, Mr Brown, and so it appears that he has no literacy problems. As the reminder letters have received no reply, Sharon should telephone Bob. During the conversation, Bob pretends that he has never received any letters from Mr Brown. He also rambled on about having no money until he can sell some livestock. At this point, Sharon sees from the file that Bob Giles not only owns the farm without a mortgage, but also has 3 new tractors which were bought with cash without the need for finance. This tends to support the view that Bob has the money and is simply delaying payment. During the conversation, Sharon should try and obtain confirmation from Bob that there is no dispute about the services provided by Mr Brown. Bob Giles says that he realises that there is a fee outstanding but was waiting to receive an invoice. Although it appears that Bob is not being entirely honest, Sharon quite rightly decides to send a letter following up the conversation by recorded delivery. Sending a letter by recorded delivery is obviously more expensive, and not necessary in every case, but in this situation it would seem appropriate. The letter encloses a copy of the invoice and makes it clear that if payment is not received within 7 days of the date of the letter, then legal action will be taken because the invoice is now overdue by 4 months.

Seven days later, Sharon checks to see that the recorded delivery letter has been signed for and then makes another call to Bob Giles. He again tries to deny having received her letter but she points out that the letter was sent by recorded delivery and that he signed for it! Bob then switches the conversation to his claim that he cannot afford to pay the bill. Armed with all the information from Bob's file, this is a clear example of where the debtor is not being truthful about his finances. Sharon should explain to Bob why she believes he is not telling the whole story. It is better to use phrases such as "I find it hard to believe", rather than saying the debtor is lying. Calling the debtor a liar is almost certain to provoke an aggressive exchange of words, which will divert you from the aim of getting the debtor to agree to pay. Also, refraining from calling the debtor a liar avoids embarrassment and reduces the chances of a complaint if you have made a mistake or do not have enough evidence to prove it.

The example of Bob Giles and RG Accountants illustrates the control a creditor has if they hold information about the debtor. If Bob Giles refuses to pay, there is a strong chance of recovering the money if court action is started.

Debt Collection Practices and the Consumer

When chasing a debtor who is an individual, care must be taken to ensure that you do not commit an offence. There are a number of pieces of legislation which debt collectors should be aware of. The most important ones are:

- The Protection from Harassment Act 1997
- Administration of Justice Act 1970 as amended
- The Office of Fair Trading Debt Collection Guidelines 2011

Section 1 of the Protection from Harassment Act 1997 states:

(1) A person must not pursue a course of conduct—
(a) which amounts to harassment of another, and

(b) which he knows or ought to know amounts to harassment of the other.

Section 3 of the PHA 1997 provides a civil remedy for anyone who is the subject of harassment. A court can grant an injunction and or award damages for (among other things) any anxiety caused by the harassment and any financial loss resulting from the harassment. As section 2 of the PHA 1997 provided for criminal liability, there was initially much discussion among lawyers as to whether Claimants pursuing a civil remedy had to show that the harassment would have engaged criminal liability before a civil claim for harassment would succeed. Recent cases have changed the position so that the claimant does not have to show the behaviour was criminal in nature before imposing civil liability. The shift away from judging civil harassment claims by the criminal benchmark was further confirmed by the case of ***Ferguson v. British Trading Ltd (2009).*** However, as the judges remarked in the case, in life we have to put up with a certain amount of annoyance and so things have to be fairly severe before the civil law can be used.

The decision in the case of ***Ferguson v British Gas Trading Ltd*** must be taken on board by organisations which use standard computer generated letters for debt collection.

<u>The facts:</u>

After switching suppliers, F continued to receive computer-issued invoices, demands for payment, and threats of being reported to credit reference agencies from her previous supplier (British Gas). Despite repeated phone calls and letters, F found it impossible to make British Gas accept that she was no longer their customer, and brought a claim for harassment. British Gas applied to have the Particulars of Claim struck out on the ground that they disclosed no reasonable grounds for bringing the claim. The High Court (Queen's Bench Division) refused the application, and British Gas appealed.

Decision:
The Court of Appeal dismissed the appeal.

Lord Justice Jacob said:

> *"Ms Ferguson claims that British Gas's course of conduct amounts to unlawful harassment contrary to the Protection from Harassment Act 1997…..*
>
> *British Gas says it has done nothing wrong; that it is perfectly all right for it to treat consumers in this way, at least if it is all just done by computer. ……*
>
> *[Counsel for British Gas] also made the point that the correspondence was computer generated and so, for some reason which I do not really follow, Ms Ferguson should not have taken it as seriously as if it had come from an individual. But real people are responsible for programming and entering material into the computer. It is British Gas's system which, at the very least, allowed the impugned conduct to happen.*
>
> *Moreover the threats and demands were to be read by a real person, not by a computer. A real person is likely to suffer real anxiety and distress if threatened in the way which Ms Ferguson was. And a real person is unlikely to take comfort from knowing that the claims and threats are unjustified or that they were sent by a computer system: that will not necessarily allay the fear that the threats will not be carried out. How is a consumer such as Ms Ferguson to know whether or not, for instance, a threat such as "we will tell a credit reference agency in the next 10 days that you have not paid" (letter of 2nd January) will not be carried out by the same computer system which sent the unjustified letter and all its predecessor bills and threats? After all no amount of*

writing and telephoning had stopped the system so far – at times it must have seemed like a monster machine out of control moving relentlessly forward – a million miles from the "world class level of service" (letter of 9th January) which British Gas says it aims to offer."

The moral of this case is that companies who use standard computer generated letters cannot simply use the excuse that it was a mere standard letter. They must be careful to ensure that the information they contain are correct and if a debtor makes contact then subsequent actions must take account of that information. Therefore, this case is likely to put the human touch back into debt collection and quell the proliferation of debt collection agencies that are merely skilled at generating a huge number of standard letters. So if you send out a chasing letter which is met with a reasoned response that they do not owe the debt, it is not advisable to continue to churn out the same letter which simply repeats a demand for payment.

In addition to the civil remedy in the PHA 1997, section 40 of The Administration of Justice Act 1970 is a very important piece of legislation that should be borne in mind when chasing non commercial debtors.

40. Punishment for unlawful harassment of debtors

(1)A person commits an offence if, with the object of coercing another person to pay money claimed from the other as a debt due under a contract, he—
(a)harasses the other with demands for payment which, in respect of their frequency or the manner or occasion of making any such demand, or of any threat or publicity by which any demand is

accompanied, are calculated to subject him or members of his family or household to alarm, distress or humiliation;
(b)falsely represents, in relation to the money claimed, that criminal proceedings lie for failure to pay it;
(c)falsely represents himself to be authorised in some official capacity to claim or enforce payment; or
(d)utters a document falsely represented by him to have some official character or purporting to have some official character which he knows it has not.

Documents issued by creditors and that resemble a court document with the intention to make the debtor believe they have come from or have the authority of the court would be in breach of section 40 of the Administration of Justice Act 1970. It is a common practice by some credit controllers or debt collection companies to send to the debtor a copy of the court claim form before it has been sent to the court office for issuing. Even if the accompanying letter states that the document is a draft of what will be sent to the court, then that could still fall foul of the law because it is liable to mislead certain people. Debt collectors also have to consider the manner and frequency with which they contact individuals.

The Office of Fair Trading has brought out guidelines for debt collectors who hold a consumer credit licence. As a result of these guidelines, debt collectors should not ignore third parties, such as Solicitors and Citizens Advice Bureau, who have been appointed by the debtor. It can also be regarded as unfair to communicate with consumers in an unclear, inaccurate or misleading manner. Some examples which are identified by these guidelines as being unfair or deceitful are:

- Use of official looking documents intended or likely to mislead debtors as to their status, for example documents which resemble court papers

- Not making it clear who you are when contacting the debtor and the purpose of the communication
- Contacting debtors at unreasonable times
- Ignoring or disregarding debtors' legitimate wishes in respect of when and where to contact them, e.g. shift workers who ask not to be contacted during the day.
- Contacting the debtors directly and bypassing their appointed representatives

There are other practices which the guidelines consider oppressive, such as:

- Acting in a way that is likely to be publicly embarrassing to the debtor, either deliberately or through lack of care, such as by not putting correspondence in a sealed envelope and putting it through a letterbox and thereby running the risk of it being read by third parties.
- Disclosing or threatening to disclose debt details to third parties unless legally entitled to do so
- Contacting the debtor at unreasonable intervals

Chapter 4

Issuing a County Court Claim

Protocols and the Letter of Claim

Before starting court proceedings, it is important to ensure that you have followed any pre-action protocols. Pre-action protocols are a series of steps each party must take before starting court proceedings. The intention of protocols is to encourage the early exchange of information which increases the chances of a settlement, or at least narrow the issues in dispute. It is in keeping with the over-riding objective where court action is regarded as the last resort.

A letter of claim should give sufficient information to identify the nature of the claim and give a reasonable opportunity to reply. The content will depend on whether the debtor is a business or an individual.

Letters of claim to Individual debtors:

The Protocol on Pre-Action Conduct is not intended to apply to debt claims where it is not disputed that the money is owed and where the claimant follows a statutory or other formal pre- action procedure. However, there is a requirement where the creditor is a business and the debtor is an individual, for the business to provide the debtor with information about sources of advice, before proceedings can be issued. Paragraph 7 of the Practice Direction deals with exchange of information before the start of proceedings and suggests that:

- A letter of claim is sent.

- The debtor should acknowledge the letter within 14 days and give a full response within a reasonable period of time, which for a straightforward undisputed debt is generally 14 days.
- Annex B to the Practice Directions sets out specific information that should be provided before starting Proceedings in a debt claim by a claimant who is a business against a defendant who is an individual. Annex B makes provision for the information a claimant business should provide to the individual debtor and this is that the claimant should:

(1) Provide details of how the money can be paid (for example the method of payment and the address to which it can be sent);
(2) State that the defendant can contact the claimant to discuss possible repayment options, and provide the relevant contact details; and
(3) Inform the defendant that free independent advice and assistance can be obtained from organisations and then provide details of these organisations

The information about where an individual can obtain advice may be provided at any time between the claimant first intimating the possibility of court proceedings and the claimant's letter before claim. It may well be that your client has provided the information to the individual debtor before you are instructed to send the letter of claim. However, even if the client has already provided the information, it would prudent to avoid any doubt and reason for a delay for the Letter of Claim to include the required information about seeking independent advice. Where the defendant is unable to provide a full response within the time specified in the letter before claim because the defendant intends to seek debt advice, then the written acknowledgment should state:

(1) That the defendant is seeking debt advice;
(2) Who the defendant is seeking advice from; and
(3) When the defendant expects to have received that advice and be in a position to provide a full response.

A claimant should allow a reasonable period of time of up to 14 days for a defendant to obtain debt advice. However, the claimant need not allow the defendant time to seek debt advice if the claimant knows that the defendant has already received relevant debt advice and the defendant's circumstances have not significantly changed or the defendant has previously asked for time to seek debt advice but has not done so.

An example of a letter of claim to a non-commercial debtor is as follows:

> *Dear Mr Smith*
> *Our Client: Big Catalogue Company Ltd*
> *Amount due: £2,000*
>
> *We are instructed by Big Catalogue Company Ltd in respect of the above outstanding account. This relates to the goods you ordered from our client and are detailed on the attached statement. This account is overdue and unless payment is received or acceptable proposals to pay are made we will issue court action.*
>
> *The account can be paid by sending a cheque payable to Big Catalogue Company at 10 Market Square, Upton, UP1 3XP or by telephoning 0800 999 666 to make a payment by debit or credit card. If you wish to discuss repayment options, please contact our client's collections department on 0800 555 444.*

We should inform you that free independent advice can be obtained from the organisations set out below:

National Debtline: FREEPHONE 0808 808 4000 www.nationaldebtline.co.uk
Consumer Credit Counselling Service: FREEPHONE 0800 138 1111 www.cccs.co.uk
Citizens Advice: CHECK YOUR LOCAL DIRECTORY for numbers and addresses
Community Legal: 0845 345 4345 www.clsdirect.org.uk

If we do not receive a response from you within 14 days of the date of this letter, then our client will start court action against you to recover the outstanding sum.

Yours sincerely

Letters of Claim to Business debtors

If the pre-action protocols are not complied with, the court has the power to penalise the offending party by imposing a costs order. However, there are situations when it would not be reasonable to expect the creditor to comply fully with the protocol. There will be many occasions in debt recovery when you will want to proceed swiftly because delaying court action could mean the debtor having no funds to settle your claim. It may be that the debtor is going to move assets out of reach or the business is in danger of collapse.

The protocol on pre-action behaviour also specifically mentions that court action should be regarded as the last resort and the parties may be required to show that they have considered alternative methods of resolving the dispute, such as mediation.

Mr Smith and Reeves Printing

Mr Smith entered into an agreement with Reeves Printing for the production of 1000 copies of his novel for the agreed price of £3,000. Payment was due by the 21 July but despite several reminders by telephone and letter from the credit controller, Reeves Printing had not had any response or payment from Mr Smith.

The legal department sends the following letter of claim to Mr Smith:

> *20 October*
> *Dear Mr Smith*
>
> ***Re: The printing of your novel***
> ***Amount Due: £3,000***
>
> *We write regarding the outstanding account concerning the printing of your novel. This debt relates to the printing and binding of 1000 copies of your book for the agreed price of £3,000 as per the contract dated the 1 June. The books were delivered to you on the 25 June and payment should have been received by the 21 July.*
>
> *Despite several reminders by the credit control department we have not received any response from you and this account remains outstanding. We are not aware of a valid reason for non-payment of this account. If you dispute that this amount is due, then please let us have your reasons in writing immediately.*
>
> *Unless payment or acceptable proposals to pay are received at the above office by* **noon on 5 November**, *we will issue court action to recover the amount due. If legal proceedings are started the court fee and a claim for interest at the rate of*

8% will be added to the amount due. Payments should be sent to the above address and cheques made payable to "Reeves Printing". Any correspondence or telephone calls regarding this matter should be addressed to Mr Nasty in the legal department.

Yours faithfully,

Mr V Nasty
Legal Department

Following the sending of the letter by Mr Nasty, Reeves Printing receives their first response from Mr Smith:

25 October

Dear Mr Nasty,

I refer to your letter of 20 October. I dispute that the amount of £3,000 is due because the books you delivered contained errors. I do not believe that I should pay for mistakes which were not my fault.

Yours sincerely,

Mr F Smith

Having received this, it would be advisable to answer the points raised before issuing court proceedings.

30 October
Dear Mr Smith,

We refer to your letter of the 25 October.

This is the first time that you have raised the issue of errors in the book after 3 months of chasing for payment. In fact, it is the first response we have had from you. We are not aware of errors in the book but even if there are mistakes, that would not be our responsibility because we merely printed the manuscript which you provided in Word format without it being edited by us. If you believe that the text in the book differs from the manuscript you submitted, please provide us with specific examples.

We must ask that you make payment of the outstanding £3,000 or put forward acceptable proposals to pay by 8 November, otherwise we will have no option but to start court proceedings.

A cheque sent in full and final settlement

It is not uncommon for debtors to send a cheque to the creditor for an amount that is less than that being claimed and saying that it is in full and final settlement. If the creditor banks the cheque can they continue to claim the balance from the debtor? The courts approach this situation by looking at all the circumstances but the general position is that if the person receiving the cheque banks it without communicating any objection or qualification to the debtor, then he will be taken to have accepted the offer and cannot recover the balance. So if the person receiving the cheque contacts the debtor before presenting it and says "we are banking the cheque on account and will be claiming the balance", then the offer has not been accepted in full and final payment and they may chase for the balance. It would be advisable to send this letter by fax if possible, with the hard copy in the post, because it is a quick method of responding and the fax transmission slip is evidence that the debtor received the letter.

Preparing to issue a court claim

The deadline passes without any reply or payment from Mr Smith. Reeves Printing now prepare to start court proceedings. Before doing so, they make a few basic checks on the financial situation of Mr Smith. They undertake a search of the Land Registry to see if he owns 18 Victoria Street, Upton. This can be done by requesting official copies of the title register for that property, provided the land is registered. The vast majority of land in England and Wales is now registered. Solicitors or other account holders can request the copies of the register by telephone. Otherwise you can complete the form and send it to the appropriate district office together with the fee of £4. Forms can be downloaded from the Land Registry website: www.landreg.gov.uk

Mr Smith is the sole owner of the property and no mortgages are registered against the property. Reeves Printing also search the Registry of County Court Judgments. This is done by sending a request to the Registry Trust Limited to search the register. The Registry Trust maintains the register of all county court judgments. The request needs to contain the full name of the person (or company), their present address and any known previous addresses, together with the period of the search, e.g. for the previous 6 years. A fee of £8 is required. The form to request a search of the register can be downloaded from the Registry Trust's website: www.registry-trust.org.uk

All county court money judgments are entered on the register and will remain there unless it is paid within one month, in which case the debtor can apply for the entry to be removed. If the judgment is paid after one month, the entry can be marked as satisfied but it will remain on the register for 6 years.

Reeves Printing discover that there are no county court judgments registered against Mr Smith. In view of this and the fact that he owns a property, if they obtain judgment then there a good chance of enforcing it (collecting the money from Mr Smith).With the knowledge that Mr Smith is not a man of straw, Reeves Printing prepare the claim ready to be sent to the local county court for issuing. Reeves Printing need to complete a claim Form (N1) which can be obtained from the court office or downloaded from the Court Service website. Reeves Printing complete the claim form as shown in Figure 3 at the end of this chapter.

Limitation Act 1980 and debt recovery

Before starting court action, consideration should be given to whether or not the debt may be statute barred. The Limitation Act 1980 provides a defence where it is more than 6 years since the debt became due on the date proceedings were issued. However, there are exceptions to this general rule, for example, where the debtor acknowledges the debt or makes part payment. So if a debt became due in June 1998, and on 1 June 2003, the debtor make a part payment of the debt, the limitation period of 6 years starts to run from June 2003 and the creditor will have until 31 May 2009 to commence court proceedings.[1]

For an acknowledgement to be effective, it must be in writing and be signed by the person making it.

Completing and Issuing a Claim Form

From 19 March 2012, there was an important change to administration of money claims. If you want to make a county court money claim you must send the claim form to the "County Court Money Claims Centre" (CCMCC) or if you don't want to use the CCMC, then you will have to use Money Claims On-Line (see

1 Section 29(5) of Limitation Act 1980.

below). This change was part of improvements to the administration of civil business. Whether it is an improvement remains to be seen. The change is not favoured by everybody in the legal profession. The move to the centralisation of court administration has its critics as many regard the local county courts as being more efficient than large national administrative centres.

Cases will be issued at the CCMCC and where they become defended and ready to be allocated to a track, they will be transferred to an appropriate county court. Claim Forms can be posted to the CCMC at:

Salford Business Centre
PO Box 527
Salford
M5 0BY

Any enquiries on cases proceeding at the CCMCC should be made to the following:

For email enquiries: ccmcccustomerenquiries@hmcts.gsi.gov.uk
For e-filing enquiries: ccmcce-filing@hmcts.gsi.gov.uk
For telephone enquiries: 0300 1231372

It is important to complete the claim form as accurately as you can. The Claim Form (N1) is shown at the end of this book in Appendix B. The Claim Form changed when the new CCMC was introduced on 19 March 2012.

Once the claim form has been served on the defendant, permission is needed from the defendant to amend it and if that is not forthcoming then you would have to apply to the court. So ensure you have entered the details correctly and that you have named the defendant correctly. If the defendant is a business then it is important to have the correct legal entity of the organisation. Is the business an incorporated company? If it is, then there should be the word "Ltd" or "Limited" after its name. A limited company should have the registered company number on its headed paper and so you can use this number to check the full company name and registered office by visiting Companies House website. It is advisable to state the registered office of a company as the address where the court should send the claim. This should remove any doubts of service. You can of course always send a copy of the claim to the trading address after the court has sent it to the registered office.

On the claim form there must be a statement of value. The statement of value should be inserted below the word "Value" on the front page of the claim form. The form of wording should be: "Value: £X plus accrued interest and fixed costs

In deciding which level of court fee the claim comes within, the court takes into account the interest claimed to the date of the claim.

In a personal injury claim, for example, where you would be claiming general damages for pain and suffering, statement of value would be worded, for example, as "the claimant expects to recover between £5,000 and £15,000".

The particulars of claim in many debt actions can be included in the space provided on the claim form. Where the particulars of a claim are more detailed, then a separate sheet should be attached. Separate particulars of claim should be headed as shown overleaf:

See overleaf.

IN THE UPTON COUNTY COURT *CLAIM No.*
Between:
Reeves Printing Ltd *(Claimant)*
And
Mr Fred Smith *(Defendant)*

Particulars of Claim

The particulars of claim should be a coherent statement of the case. In the case of Reeves Printing, it is a claim for the agreed price of printing and binding 1000 copies of Mr Smith's book. The particulars of the claim by Reeves Printing are set out on the claim form in Figure 3. Practice Direction 16 of the CPR states that certain matters must be included in the particulars of claim. Where a claim is based upon a written agreement, the contract or documents forming the agreement should be attached to the particulars of claim. In the case of Reeves Printing, the contract signed on the 1 June is attached to the particulars of claim.

The claim by Reeves Printing includes a claim for interest. The entitlement to claim interest can arise in the following ways:

- According to a clause in the contract.
- According to the Late Payment of Commercial Debts (Interest) Act 1998, as amended and supplemented by The Late Payment of Commercial Debt Regulations 2002. From the 7 August 2002, interest under the Late Payment legislation applies to businesses of whatever size. There are also provisions to claim fixed amounts of compensation depending on the size of the debt. This was set out in Chapter 1. The rate of interest is 8% per cent above the base rate. The reference level is set and

prevails for a six-month period. So, for example, from the 1 January 2009 to the 30 June 2009, the reference base rate was 2% and so the rate of interest that could be claimed under this legislation was 10%. To check the current rate, visit: www.payontime.co.uk

- According to section 69 of the County Courts Act 1984 at the rate of 8%.

Figure 3 shows that you must state on the claim form not only the amount of interest from the date the debt became due to the date of the claim, but also the daily rate at which interest will continue to accrue. Reeves Printing would not be able to claim interest under the Late Payment legislation because Mr Smith is not acting in the course of a business, although that may be an arguable point if he is a professional writer. In this situation, Mr Smith is merely writing in his spare time and his regular occupation is that of a civil servant.

The particulars of claim must be verified by a statement of truth. The person signing a statement of truth can be guilty of contempt of court if they know that the facts contained within the document are untrue. A solicitor can sign the statement of truth on behalf of his client. The solicitor signs the statement of truth in his own name but states that: *"The Claimant believes…."*. A solicitor should check the contents of the particulars of claim with his client before he signs it on their behalf. If the statement of truth is being signed by an officer of a company, that person must be of a senior level, such as a manager or director.

On the front page of the claim form, there are boxes where you enter the amount of the claim. There is a box for fixed solicitors' costs as allowed by the court rules. These fixed costs can only be claimed if you have a solicitor acting for you.

There is a court fee to issue a court claim. The level of fee depends on the amount claimed. The latest court fees can be obtained from the Court Service website. If a case is defended and progresses to a hearing then there will be further fees to pay. The following shows the further fees payable depending on the track the case is allocated to:

Small Claims Track	Allocation Fee (if claim over 1,500)	Hearing Fee	
Fast Track	Allocation Fee	Listing Fee	Hearing Fee
Multi Track	Allocation Fee	Listing Fee	Hearing Fee

The current policy of the Ministry of Justice is to make county courts self-financing which has caused a steady increase in court fees. If you are an individual and are either on a qualifying state benefit or your disposable income is below a certain level, you may be able to obtain a full or part fee remission, which means that you will not have to pay all or part of the required court fee. To claim for a "fee remission", you will have to complete the relevant application form and supply up to date documentary evidence regarding your finances. Fee remissions are not available for businesses.

If a claim is issued through the Claim Production Centre, then the court fee is discounted. The Claim Production Centre is designed for those issuing a large number of debt actions.

Freezing Orders

A creditor can prevent a debtor from moving assets out of reach by applying for a freezing order. A freezing order is an injunction which prevents a party from removing assets out of the country or from dealing with the assets. Applications for a freezing injunction are usually made to the High Court, but there are exceptions where an order can be granted by a county court such as where it is sought to aid execution after judgment. If you are considering applying for a freezing order, it is strongly recommended that you seek the assistance of a solicitor.

Making a Claim Online

Those with access to the internet can start a claim for money online. To start the claim, you need to visit the Court Service website: www.moneyclaim.gov.uk/web/mcol/welcome

With the introduction of the new County Court Money Claims Centre on 19 March 2012, the use of Money Claim Online is expected to increase. This was probably one of the intentions of introducing a centralised "back office". The issuing of claims online has its attractions. The service is open to individuals, solicitors and companies. It has the advantage that it operates 24 hours a day, 7 days a week and so you can go online anytime and monitor the progress of your case. Also, a change to the court rules that came into force in April 2009 enables more detailed particulars of claim to be served separately within 14 days of issuing the claim. This removed the disadvantage of the online claim form having limited space for giving particulars of the claim.

To use "Money Claims Online", the claim has to be for a fixed amount that is less than £100,000. You have to pay for the court fees by credit or debit card. Users of this system cannot obtain an exemption from court fees

Serving the Claim

Where the defendant gives an address for service within the jurisdiction, the defendant may be served with the claim form at that address. If the defendant has given the address of a solicitor within the jurisdiction or the solicitor has notified the claimant that he is instructed to accept service, the claim form must be served at the business address of that solicitor. Where the defendant does not give an address for service and the claimant does not wish to effect personal service, the claim form must be served on the defendant at the place shown in the table below:

Nature of defendant to be served	**Place of service**
1.Individual	Usual or last known address
2.Individual being sued in the name of a business	Usual or last known residence of the individual or principal or last known place of business
3.Individual being sued in the business name of a partnership	Principal office of the partnership or principal or last known place of business of the partnership
4.Limited Liability Partnership	Principal office of the partnership or any place within the jurisdiction which has a real connection with the claim
5.Company registered in England or Wales	Principal office of the company or any place of business of the company within the jurisdiction which has a real connection with the claim
6.Corporation (other than a company) incorporated in England or Wales	Principal office of the corporation or any place within the jurisdiction where the corporation carries on its activities and which has a real connection with the claim
7.Any other company or corporation	Any place within the jurisdiction where the corporation carries on its activities or any place of business of the company within the jurisdiction.

Where a claimant has reason to believe that the address of the defendant is an address at which the defendant no longer resides or carries on business, the claimant must take reasonable steps to find the address of the defendant's current residence or place of business. Having taken reasonable steps to find the current address, the claim form must be served at that address. If the claimant is unable to find the defendant's current address, the claimant must consider whether there is an alternative place where, or an alternative method by which the service may be effected. If the claimant cannot find the current residence or place of business and cannot ascertain an alternative place or an alternative method of service, then the claimant may serve on the defendant's usual or last known address.

A claim form is deemed to be served on the second business day after completion of the relevant step under Part 7.5(1). Part 7.5 states that where the claim form is served within the jurisdiction, the claimant must complete the step required by the following table in relation to the particular method of service chosen, before 12.00 midnight on the calendar day four months after the date of issue of the claim form.

Method of Service	Step Required
First class post, document exchange or other service which provides for delivery on the next business day	Posting, leaving with, delivering to or collection by relevant service provider
Delivery of the document to or leaving it at the relevant place	Delivering to or leaving the document at the relevant place
Personal service	A claim form is served personally on: -an individual by leaving it with that individual; -a company or other corporation by leaving it with a person holding a senior position within the company

	or corporation; -a partnership (where partners are being sued in the name of their firm) by leaving it with a partner or a person who, at the time of service, has the control or management of the partnership at its principal place of business
Fax	Completing the transmission of the fax
Other electronic method	Sending the e mail or other electronic communication

The defendant may respond in one of the following ways:

- defend the claim
- admit the claim
- admit part of the claim

The defendant will have 14 days from the date of service in which to respond to the claim. If the defendant completes the acknowledgement of service form indicating an intention to defend, then they have 28 days from the date of service in which to file a defence. So if the claim was deemed to have been served on the 2 September and the defendant files an acknowledgement of service by 16 September, saying he intends to defend the claim, then he has until 4pm on the 30 September to file a defence.

If a defendant admits the claim it is likely that they will request time to pay. The claimant has the opportunity to object to the rate of payment being offered by the defendant. If they do, the rate will be decided by a court official. The claimant can object to the determination by applying to a District Judge, if they feel it is too low. Should the financial circumstances of the defendant change, it is open for the claimant to apply to the court for a variation order, by completing form N244, stating the reasons why the defendant should be ordered to pay more. Of course, it is open to the defendant to apply to the court to vary the order downwards.

When a defendant admits part of the claim, the claimant can either accept the part admission as settlement of the claim or reject it and continue with the case. The claimant cannot accept the part admission and still continue the claim in respect of the balance.

The Debtor Defends the Claim

Since the changes to the civil procedure rules brought about by Woolf, the county courts should take a more active role in filtering out defences which clearly do not show valid grounds for defending the claim. Where the court office believes there is a defect in the defence, it will be referred to a District Judge for a decision. The court should pull out defences which are merely a bare denial and refer it to a Judge who is likely to give directions that unless the defendant files a properly pleaded defence by a certain date, the defence will be struck out and judgment entered for the claimant. If the claimant receives a defence which simply says "I deny the claim" then they should write to the court asking that it makes an order of its own initiative and strike out the defence. The court should not charge a fee to exercise its own initiative.

The letter to the court should read as follows:

We refer to the Defence received from the Defendant. The Defence is a bare denial of the Claim and we ask the Court to exercise its powers under CPR Part 3.3 and make an Order of its own initiative and strike out the Defence as it shows no reasonable grounds for defending.

In the case of Reeves Printing, Fred Smith enters the following defence:

"*I dispute that the money is due because the books which Reeves Printing delivered contained errors and were in a poor condition. I should not have to pay for books which were not of satisfactory quality because of a number of printing errors and the fact that the books were so badly bound that pages quickly fell out.*"

Summary Judgment

It seems that Fred Smith has entered a time wasting defence. The fact that no response was received from him until the letter before court action, casts doubt on the merits of his defence. If there were serious problems with the book, then why was there no contact from Fred Smith shortly after receiving delivery of the books? Further, if when he refers to errors he means mistakes in the manuscript, then it is unlikely to be the fault of Reeves Printing because he supplied the text on a computer disk in Word format and they printed it without any editing. Also, Reeves Printing did invite Mr Smith to provide examples of where the book allegedly differs from the manuscript he submitted but he has given no details of any errors. Therefore, Reeves Printing could consider an application for summary judgment.

Under Part 24 of the CPR, a claimant (or defendant) can apply for summary judgment if they believe that the other party has no real prospect of success and that there is no other compelling reason for a trial. To apply for summary judgment, form N244 needs to be completed and sent to the court office with the application fee. Form N244 is shown in Appendix A. The court will set a date for the application to be heard. Reeves Printing must file at the court and serve on Mr Smith the evidence they wish to rely on at least 7 days before the hearing.

An application for summary judgment is not intended to be a mini-trial. If there are issues which would involve witness evidence, then it is likely that a judge would consider that it is appropriate to set it down for a full trial. The question is what is meant by "real prospect of success"? The courts have decided that where the defence is fanciful, then summary judgment should be granted. A clear example of this would be where a debtor in open correspondence says they are unable to settle an account because of financial difficulties, but when a court claim is issued they raise an argument that the goods were defective. Therefore, the meaning of "fanciful" is where a case has no substance and is contradicted by all the documents or other material. In the case of Reeves Printing, the argument by Fred Smith regarding errors may not have a realistic prospect of success but the point about the badly bound books is not so fanciful, although it is surprising that this issue was first raised in the defence. If a judge is not satisfied that summary judgment should be granted, then he might order that the defendant only be allowed to defend on certain conditions, such as providing a more detailed defence. It is also likely that the judge will give an individual the benefit of the doubt particularly if they are not legally represented and not enter summary judgment. If the defendant is a business, then summary judgment is more likely to be granted because judges take the view that a company should be more commercially aware and should have taken legal advice.

It should be borne in mind that if you make an application for summary judgment, the court still requires payment of the allocation fee even though allocation will not take place if the application is successful. This is another indication of some court fees being mere revenue raisers rather than reflecting work done. Some courts have been known to await the outcome of the application for summary judgment and if it fails, then require payment of the allocation fee forthwith.

In addition, it may not always be worth making an application for summary judgment where the claim falls within the small claims limit because the hearing of a small claim is usually listed within 2 to 3 months of completing the allocation questionnaire. So a small claim in many cases proceeds to trial much more quickly than in the fast track or multi-track and so it may not be worth paying an additional court fee to attempt to obtain judgment a few weeks earlier. For a long time, the summary judgment procedure was not available in small claims but this was changed with the introduction of the CPR after the Woolf reforms.

It is advisable to use the summary judgment procedure only where it is quite clear from the face of the documents that the defence (or claim) does not have a real prospect of success and the hearing is not going to take longer than 30 minutes. Perhaps the best use of the summary judgment procedure is where the debtor has admitted in open correspondence that the debt is due but later denies the claim in his defence.

Settling a claim after the issue of court action

The debtor will often approach the creditor to settle the matter after a court claim has arrived in their letter box. If the offer to settle is acceptable, the creditor should ensure that some kind of written agreement is signed so that if the debtor fails to keep to his promise then the creditor can restore the court action to enforce what was agreed. The creditor should not simply withdraw the court claim because if the debtor fails to pay as agreed, the creditor would have to start a fresh action. The creditor should apply for a "consent order" whereby the action is stayed pending the carrying out of the terms to settle the dispute. Where lawyers are representing the parties then a formal consent order will be drawn up and sent to the court. The court will usually charge a fee to formally make an order on the terms agreed. The benefit of having such an Order (which lawyers describe as a "Tomlin Order") is that if the debtor defaults on the agreement, then you can apply to court to enforce the Order. The creditor should of course request that the debtor pay this court fee. The wording of such an order is shown below:

In the Upton County Court   Case No UP00001

Between:
Reeves Publishing Ltd (Claimant)
And
Fred Smith   (Defendant)

Consent Order

Upon the parties having agreed the terms set out in the schedule

IT IS ORDERED BY CONSENT:

1. *All proceedings in this action are stayed except for the purpose of enforcing the terms agreed in the Schedule below and either party may apply to court to enforce the agreed terms.*
2. *There be no order as to costs*

SCHEDULE:

a. The Defendant do pay the sum of £2,000 to the Defendant in full settlement of this claim by way of instalments of £400 per month with the first instalment due on the ________ and thereafter on the _____ day of each month until.

b. If the Defendant does not pay as agreed in paragraph a, then the Claimant may enter Judgment for £2,000 without further Order.

In situations where the debtor is not represented the drawing up of a formal consent order may not be so easy, but the creditor should at least try and get the debtor to confirm the offer in writing. It would be sensible for the creditor to send a letter to the debtor setting out the terms of the agreement and requesting the debtor to sign and send back a copy. The creditor can then send this to the court requesting that the matter be stayed as the case has been settled. Suppose that Mr Smith makes an offer to settle the claim of Reeves Printing by proposing to pay £2,000 in full and final settlement by instalments of £400 per month. Reeves Printing should send the following to Mr Smith:

Dear Mr Smith,

Reeves Printing v. Mr John Smith Claim No. UP00000

We refer to our telephone conversation on the xx/xx/xx when you made the offer to settle this claim by paying £2,000 in full and final settlement of the claim by Reeves Printing to be paid by instalments of £400 per month. The first instalment is to be paid on the 1st of January xxxx and thereafter on the first day of each month.

We accept your offer to settle this claim. We will write to the court and request that the court action be stayed as the above settlement has been be reached, but if you fail to pay as agreed then we will ask the court to restore the action so that we can enforce the terms of the agreement. Please sign the copy of this letter to indicate that these are the terms of settlement and return to this office. We will then forward the signed agreement to the court.

Yours sincerely,

Mr V Nasty

Reeves Printing

Where a valid defence has been filed, the court will send out an allocation questionnaire for both parties to complete. How to deal with a defended claim and prepare the case for trial is explained in the next chapter.

Chapter 5

Taking a Defended Debt Action to Trial

Allocating a Claim

Every defended claim is allocated to one of 3 tracks:

- Small claims track;
- Fast Track; or
- Multi-track

To assist the court, the parties are usually required to complete and file an allocation questionnaire in form N150, unless the value of the claim is below the small claims limit, where a modified form N149 is used. The allocation questionnaire is required to be filed at court within 14 days of it being served. Where the claim is more than £1,500, the claimant will have to pay an allocation fee. Where the claim is for more than £5,000, the allocation fee is higher.

The allocation questionnaire asks for information on various areas including:

- *Do you wish there to be a one-month stay to attempt settlement either by informal discussion or alternative dispute resolution?*
- *Do you wish to try mediation?*
- *Is there any reason why your claim needs to be heard at any particular court?*
- *What amount of the claim is in dispute?*
- *So far as you know, what witnesses of fact do you intend to call at the trial or final hearing?*

- *Do you wish to use expert evidence at the trial?*
- *Which track to you consider most suitable for your claim? (small/fast/multi-track)*
- *How long do you estimate the trial or final hearing will take?*

For most debt claims, there will not be the need for expert evidence. To have expert evidence at a trial will require permission of the court. The litigant in person will probably not know how long a trial will last. It is probably always better to slightly over-estimate. Many small claims usually do not last more than 2 hours; many might be disposed of within an hour.

The primary factor in allocating a claim is the financial value. In February 2012, the Government announced major changes to civil litigation. One of the important proposals is to increase the small claim track limit to £10,000 from the £5,000 which existed at the time this book went to press[2]. There is an intention to further increase this to £15,000. The Fast Track relates to matters above the small claim limit up to £25,000. Above £25,000, cases will normally be in the multi-track. However, under the new proposals a district judge may decide to allocate a cases that would be in in the fast track to the small claims track.

ADR/Mediation and small claims track cases

The increase in the small claims track would mean that small business would not be in position to claim legal costs of claiming reasonably large sums of money. Not only is there to be an increase in the small claims limit but there will be the automatic transfer of small claim to mediation. This will most likely be telephone mediation which operates in cases allocated to the small claims track where the parties both agree to mediation. Alternative Dispute

---

[2] June 2012. It is not known when the changes are to be implemented

Resolution and mediation features heavily in the court rules. Parties involved in civil disputes are expected to try to resolve a dispute without going to court. The reality is that successive governments do not want to fund the county court and there is pressure on litigants to settle for something less than they are entitled to relieve the pressure on the courts.

Where a debtor has refused to discuss the matter, then mediation is unlikely to be of benefit if there is nothing to discuss. The current policy of encouraging parties to use mediation is part of the Department of Constitutional Affairs policy to reduce the number of cases going to court. It is easy to understand why creditors feel that mediation and other forms of ADR merely delay matters, giving the debtor more time to pay or avoid paying altogether. Although it is an unjust system, it appears that creditors are going to have to factor ADR into the process of collecting money through the courts. When chasing a small debt which becomes defended, it will in future be worth considering what you would settle for if the debt was paid quickly rather than go to a small claims hearing which would involve paying further court hearing fees and having to wait longer to get paid. To illustrate, a strategy that might be adopted in small claims that are referred to mediation is set out below in the case of *GT Marketing Ltd v LDF Recruitment Ltd.*

GT issued a claim against LDF for non payment of invoices for marketing services totalling £4,500. LDF enters a defence that they believe that the marketing material was not of a satisfactory quality. The case gets referred to small claims mediation. Although GT believes it has a strong case, rather than pay further court hearing fees and wait a long time for a hearing to be listed, which in a busy court list could be several months down the line, it might be worth GT considering agreeing to settle if LDF paid a sizeable amount of the sum claimed within a short period of time. So it might wish to say to the mediator that calls to discuss the case that if LDF were to pay say 75% of the debt within 14 days, then GT would discontinue it claim. An agreement could be drawn up to say: "In consideration of LDF paying the sum of £3,375.00 within 14 days of the date of this agreement, GT agrees to discontinue its claim against LDF. If LDF does not pay in accordance with the terms of this agreement, GT will be permitted to enter Judgment without further Order"

Although the heavy pressure to push parties to a dispute to accept less than what they entitled to receive is a result of unfair Government policy, doing a deal at an early stage as illustrated in the case of GT Marketing may be appropriate where you want to maintain cash flow and avoid paying further court fees which may not be recovered. It may also be the case that getting what you can early on is advantageous because in a perilous economic climate the defendant may go under by the time the case comes to be decided.

Court Directions

The Small Claims Track

Once a hearing is set, a court hearing fee will be payable within 14 days. The current level of court hearing fees for small claims is as follows:

Hearing Fee (small claims track)	
Claim does not exceed £300	£25
Claim exceeds £300 but under £500	£55

Claim exceeds £500 but under £1,000	£80
Claim exceeds £1,000 but under £1,500	£110
Claim exceeds £1,500 but under £3,000	£165
Claim exceeds £3,000	£325

It should be remembered that if court hearing fees are not paid, then the court will strike out the claim.

Directions are a series of steps to prepare the case for the hearing. If a party does not comply with a direction, the court may strike out that party's case. The court will usually issue an "unless order" before actually striking out a case. The standard directions for a small claim are:

- Each party to deliver to every other party and to the court office, copies of all documents on which he intends to rely at the hearing no later than 14 days before the hearing.
- The original documents shall be brought to the hearing

A recent change to the court rules means that the district judge has to consider whether or not it would be of benefit to require the preparation of formal witness statements. This means that the court directions for small claims will not always contain a requirement to file and serve witness statements. The district judge also has the power to request that either party files further details of their case. It is believed that this will be a more common direction in small claims if a district judge requires more information about the case, rather than witness statements. Where witness statements are required, it includes statements from the claimant and defendant; the particulars of claim or defence will not be regarded as witness statements.

In a small claim, the strict rules of evidence do not apply. If a witness is not able to attend a small claims hearing, the judge may allow a signed witness statement to stand as that witness's evidence. However, the judge will give the evidence the appropriate weight bearing in mind that the witness is not there to answer questions. There are provisions in the small claims procedure for a party, who gives at least 7 days notice to the court and the other side, to request that the court decide the case in their absence taking into account all the documents that have been filed. There are also rules in the small claims procedure to allow a case to be decided without a hearing if both parties agree.

In view of the "no legal costs rule" and only very limited fixed costs for the attendance of witnesses, it is likely that many small debt actions will be decided by the judge reading the papers filed at court. It unlikely to be cost effective to have a witness travel a long way for a small claims hearing when that witness may only receive a small amount for loss of earnings and travel expenses. It is therefore unlikely that a witness is going to be willing to give up their time unless the hearing is local. It is possible to ensure the attendance of a witness by serving a witness summons. A witness summons is issued by completing form N20 and sending two copies to the court with the court fee. The summons is then served on the witness together with a sum that is reasonably sufficient to cover the cost of travelling and compensation for loss of time. If a witness does not obey a witness summons, they will be in contempt of court and can be fined up to £1,000.

In the case of Reeves Printing and Fred Smith, the documents which Reeves Publishing should exchange and file at court would include:

- The contract signed on the 1 June 2003
- The correspondence between Reeves Printing and Fred Smith
- The finished book
- Witness Statement of Robert Inkjet

Although the court directions in small claims may not always require the preparation of witness statements, in this case as in many, it will assist the judge to more quickly establish the issues. Witness statements, including the evidence of the parties, must be in the format prescribed by the court rules.

They should be set out as below:

On behalf of the Claimant:
1st
Deponent: R Inkjet
Exhibit Initials: RI1
Date:

In the Upton County Court ***Claim No. UP100000***
Between:
Reeves Printing Ltd
(Claimant)
And

Mr Fred Smith *(Defendant)*

WITNESS STATEMENT OF ROBERT INKJET

I, Robert Inkjet, of Reeves Publishing Ltd, 10 Market Place, Upton will say as follows:

1. I am employed by Reeves Printing as the production manager. I am responsible for the printing and binding of books. I am authorised to make this statement on behalf of the Claimant and the facts are those within my own knowledge. Where they are not, the source of my belief is given..

2. I was contacted by Fred Smith in May 2003 and asked for a quote for the cost of printing and binding 1000 copies of a novel he had written. I quoted a price of £3,000 and explained to Mr Smith that this service did not include editing the manuscript. Mr Smith confirmed that this was acceptable and that he would submit his manuscript. I told him that I would send out a formal contract for him to sign and return before we started the project. I received his manuscript on 7/6/2003 in Word format together with the signed contract.

3. I ....

STATEMENT OF TRUTH
I believe that the facts in this witness statement are true
I am duly authorised to make this statement

Signed *Date*
Robert Inkjet (Production Manager)

Fast Track

If the value of the claim is greater than £5,000[3] but not exceeding £25,000 and the hearing is not likely to last for more than a day, then the claim will usually be allocated to the fast track. There are

3 Soon to be £10,000

usually more directions which will be made on allocation to this track. It will involve more procedural steps than the small claims track. The normal rules of evidence apply and the succeeding party is able to recover legal costs from the losing party. The standard directions for the fast track are:

- Disclosure within 4 weeks
- Exchange of witness statements within 10 weeks
- Exchange of experts reports within 14 weeks
- Listed for trial to take place within 30 weeks of being allocated to the fast track
- The date of the trial will be in a "trial window" (not exceeding 3 weeks)

Disclosure is where you are required to disclose the documents on which you rely and the documents which adversely affect your own case or adversely affect another party's case. Sometimes the court will order the disclosure of other documents. The duty to disclose documents is limited to documents which are or have been in your control. The procedure for disclosure is that each party completes a list of documents on form N265 and serves it on the other. When making standard disclosure, a party must sign a disclosure statement. There is no requirement in small claims to complete a list of documents. The method of inspecting the documents is usually achieved by each party sending to the other copies of the documents on the list.

Stricter rules of evidence are applied in the fast track and multi-track and therefore it is important that witness statements are prepared correctly. A witness statement should be set out in the own words of the witness and expressed in the first person. The statement should follow a chronological sequence. It should identify which statements are made from information within his knowledge and the source of the information or belief. The statement deals with facts experienced first hand by the witness and should avoid opinions or legal arguments. Each paragraph should be numbered and deal with each distinct portion of the subject matter. Any documents referred to should be formally exhibited to the statement.

Multi-Track

The multi-track is for cases with a value of more than £25,000 and cases that involve difficult points of law and fact. Cases in the multi-track are more likely to have active case management by courts. Less complicated cases are likely to be given standard directions which are similar to the fast track.

In both the fast track and multi-track, the court will require a listing questionnaire to be completed before the hearing date which has the purpose of ensuring that all directions have been complied with and the availability of witnesses, experts and lawyers. There are further court fees to be paid at the time of filing the listing questionnaire.

In many cases, it is suitable for small businesses to conduct a small claim without a lawyer. However, because of the greater procedural steps and stricter rules of evidence, it is sensible to have legal representation where the debt action falls within the fast or multi-track. With legal costs generally being awarded to the winning party in the fast and multi- tracks, it is also economic to employ a solicitor. Of course, you are at risk of being liable for the legal costs of the other side if you lose a case in the fast or multi-track.

The hearing of a small debt claim

The focus of this chapter is on the making a small debt claim. Most businesses and individuals should be capable of conducting a small claim. The court rules permit a company to be represented by an officer or employee of the company. The person that represents the organisation should be someone of suitable seniority and experience.

When you arrive at the court, check in at the desk with the court usher. He will mark on the case list that you are present. Sit in the waiting area until your case is called. Be prepared for a long wait. Courts are well known for running over their schedule times. It may be that in the waiting area the defendant comes over and makes an offer to settle the case. If this happens, it would be wise to set out the terms that you have agreed in a written document. It is useful to do this because if your opponent goes back on the offer to settle, you have a legally enforceable agreement. Such a document should always include a clause that if the defendant fails to do as promised, the court case can be restored.

When your case is called, the court usher will show you into the district judge's chambers. Make sure that your mobile phone is switched off! The claimant normally sits on the right hand side of the table as you look at the judge. The general rule is that all cases are in open court, even those in chambers, unless the judge orders the hearing to be in private. Possession hearings are in private and other cases which involve personal financial matters. However, the reality is that the only people at a small claims hearing will be the parties involved simply because the judge's chambers will not have room to seat spectators. The district judge should be addressed as sir or madam. He (or she) will then make a note of each party and any representatives that are present. The district judge will have already read the papers on the court file. It is therefore important that you clearly expressed your case in the particulars of claim and other documents so that the judge will already have a good understanding of the issues.

The procedure followed at the hearing will vary depending on the district judge. The court rules permit the district judge to adopt any procedure he considers fair. If both parties are legally represented, matters may proceed in a more formal way with short opening speeches, followed by evidence and then closing speeches. Where litigants are not represented, the district judge will assess the situation and decide what he or she needs to hear in order to do justice and to ensure that the parties feel they received a fair hearing.

Preparing and presenting your case

When the judge asks you to put your case, you should have prepared a concise opening statement which outlines your claim and states what you are seeking from the defendant. It is a good idea to keep an eye on the judge's reaction as you speak. You should be able to gauge whether the judge wants you to draw your remarks to a close. Avoid rambling on about irrelevant matters or exchanging insults with your opponent. If the defendant becomes disruptive, such as interrupting, compose yourself and do not retaliate. It may work to your advantage. If you stay calm and stick to the evidence, then any bad behaviour by the defendant may mean that the district judge forms a bad impression of your opponent.

It will help your presentation if you prepare an indexed bundle of the documents to be used at the hearing. Provide copies for the judge and your opponent. You will immediately find favour with the judge if he can easily find the documents you refer to in your case.

To illustrate how to prepare and present your case, consider the case study involving Carol and Clifford. Although this example is not a commercial debt, the guidance given for the preparation and presentation of a case will also apply to a small business going to a small claims hearing.

Case Study: Carol and Clifford

In January 2000, Carol enters into a relationship with Clifford. They do not get married but after a courtship of 6 months, Carol moves in with Clifford. Clifford is an accountant and at that time, his accountancy practice was going through a difficult period. He asks Carol if she could lend him £4,000 because he needed the cash to pay his daughter's school fees. Carol pays him the money in April 2000 and says that he can repay it in 12 months time. The relationship between Carol and Clifford breaks down after 15 months in July 2001 and Carol asks Clifford to repay what she regarded as a loan. Clifford refuses as he claims it was a gift. Carol does not pursue this debt for some time but in January 2005 she is in financial difficulty and so Carol employs a debt collection agency called "Easy Money" to chase Clifford for the unpaid loan. In a telephone conversation between Mrs Chaser of Easy Money and Clifford, he agrees to repay the debt at £500 per month. Mrs Chaser confirms the conversation in writing to Clifford. Clifford makes a payment in February 2005 but then stops paying. Carol takes no further action until July 2007. Clifford refuses to pay and so Carol issues a claim in Upton County Court for the balance of £3,500 plus interest on 1 August 2007. Clifford disputes the claim saying that it was a loan and alleges that her claim is outside the limitation period of 6 years.

Carol has to show that on the balance of probability the payment of £4,000 was a loan and not a gift. The other issue is whether her claim is statute barred. Even if she did make a loan, Clifford will argue that the claim has been brought more than 6 years after April 2001. The counter argument is that under section 29 of the Limitation Act 1980, acknowledging a debt and making part payments have the effect of renewing the limitation period from the date of acknowledgment or payment. Clifford made a payment on 1

February 2005, which would renew the limitation period from that date.

In a case such as Carol and Clifford, the court is likely to make the direction that each party should produce to the court and the other party signed witness statements of the oral evidence they will give at the hearing. Although the requirement to prepare witness statements is used less frequently in small claims, the case of Carol and Clifford revolves around what was said and so a statement from the parties as to the oral evidence they will give will assist the court and probably save time. The evidence that Carol should present to the court includes:

1. Oral evidence from herself as to the circumstances surrounding the payment of £4,000
2. Oral evidence from Mrs Chaser of the telephone conversation in January 2005
3. Letter from Mrs Chaser sent to Clifford confirming the conversation in January 2005.

The following is an example of what might be said at the hearing:

Carol:
"Sir, my claim is for the sum of £3,500 which is the balance of the amount I loaned to Mr Jones in April 2000. I trust that you have read my statement that I filed at court?

District Judge:
I have glanced at the statement before the hearing but please take me through the main points.

Carol:
As you can see, in March 2000 we had discussed the fact that Mr Jones was going through financial difficulties and was finding it

hard to pay his daughter's school fees. I said that I would be happy to lend him the money and he could pay me back in 12 months time without interest. It was not until our relationship came to an end in July 2001 that I asked for the repayment of the loan. He said that he would repay me at the end of the month, which he did not. I later instructed Easy Money debt collection agency to pursue him and as you can see from the statement of Mrs Chaser, he agreed in January 2005 to repay me at £500 per month and indeed made a payment in February 2005 but nothing further.

District Judge:
Thank you Ms Smith. Mr Jones, I see that you do not deny receiving the £4,000 but say that it was a loan?

Clifford:
That is correct Sir. I was finding my finances a little tight at the time and Carol wanted to go on holiday to Barbados. She said book the holiday on my credit card and she would pay the card bill when it came in. There was nothing mentioned that it being a loan.

District Judge:
Mr Jones, but can you explain why you made a payment of £500 following a conversation you had with Mrs Chaser of Easy Money?

Clifford:
I made the payment of £500 as I had heard thorough a mutual friend that Carol was having financial difficulty and felt sympathy for her and so sent the money. I dispute that I said to Mr Chaser that I owed £4,000 to Carol or that I would pay £500 per month.

District Judge:
Then why did Mrs Chaser write a letter to you confirming the conversation?

Clifford:
I have never received such a letter.

District Judge:
Ms Smith, would you like to ask Mr Jones any questions?

Carol:
Yes, I would. Clifford, why did you pay me £500 in February 2005 if, as you allege, you never made any agreement with Mrs Chaser of Easy Money?

Clifford:
I heard through a mutual acquaintance that you were having money problems and I thought you could do with the money.

Carol:
Who was this "mutual acquaintance"?

Clifford:
I don't recall his name.

District Judge:
Mr Jones, do you wish to ask Ms Smith any questions?

Clifford:
No sir.

District Judge:
In which case, I will now give my judgment.
In the case of Carol Smith v Clifford Jones, it is likely that the Judge would give his decision straightaway. In view of the evidence presented by both parties, it is likely that the district judge would find as follows:

"This is a claim by Ms Carol Smith for the sum of £3,500 which she asserts is the balance due on a loan she made to Mr Clifford Jones in April 2000. Mr Jones in his Defence has claimed that the money was a gift. I am satisfied on the balance of probabilities that Ms Smith loaned Mr Jones the money. Mr Jones has further argued that the claim by Ms Smith was brought outside the limitation period. Ms Smith has presented the evidence of Mrs Chaser from Easy Money that Mr Jones entered into an agreement to repay the loan at £500 per month and in February 2005 she received £500. I am satisfied on the balance of probabilities that the payment of £500 made by Mr Jones was not a gift but was in fact the first instalment in respect of the agreement he reached with Mrs Chaser of Easy Money. Therefore, the payment of £500 in February was an acknowledgment of the debt and I find that the limitation period started to run from February 2005 and so the claim by Ms Smith is not outside the limitation period. I therefore grant judgment for Claimant in the sum of £3,500 plus court fees and interest. Ms Smith, what is the amount of interest? [Ms Smith gives the judge the figure]. The judgment is to be paid within 14 days."

Interest on judgments

Interest is payable on a county court judgment under the County Courts (Interest on Judgment Debts) Order 1991 (SI 1991/1184) at the rate of 8% where the judgment is not less than £5,000. Interest will apply to judgments less than £5,000 where the interest claimed was pursuant to a clause in a contract. Where a judgment creditor takes enforcement proceedings, accrual of interest ceases from that point unless the enforcement proceedings fail. Applying for a charging order is not regarded as enforcement proceedings.

Chapter 6

Collecting Your Money after a Court Judgment

Obtaining a court judgment is often the easy part of debt recovery. The debtor may simply have ignored the court claim and so the judgment was obtained in default of a response. Even if the debtor has the money to satisfy the judgment, it can still be a difficult and lengthy process to enforce the award (i.e. collect the money from the debtor). This chapter examines the various methods of enforcing a judgment and considers the most appropriate procedure according to the circumstances of the case.

What many creditors forget is that the court does not start enforcement action of its own accord; it has to be instructed by the creditor on the appropriate application form. Taking enforcement action will incur further court fees, but they are added to the debt and so are recoverable. Where there is a solicitor acting for the creditor, there are fixed solicitors costs which the court rules allow to be added to the debt.

A business which knows its customers well should be able to utilise this information to improve the chances of recovering their money. The relevance of the earlier discussion about credit checking and obtaining information about a potential new customer will now become apparent. The information should assist in deciding the most appropriate method of enforcement.

The main methods of enforcement are:

- County Court Bailiffs and High Court Enforcement Officers

- Third Party Debt Orders
- Attachment of Earnings Orders
- Charging Orders and Orders for Sale
- Orders to Attend Questioning

Strictly speaking, charging orders and orders to attend questioning are not forms of enforcement. A charging order secures a debt against property and an order for sale is then needed to realise the money. An order to attend questioning is used where you may not have sufficient information about the debtor's finances and this procedure requires the debtor to attend court and answer questions and bring documentary evidence of finances.

Bailiffs and High Court Enforcement Officers

Although Bailiffs and High Court Enforcement Officers (HCEO's and formerly known as "Sheriffs") have limited powers of entry, in the right circumstances and using the right HCEO, there is a reasonable prospect of recovery. HCEO's can enforce where the Judgment debt is at least £600. If a judgment debt is above £5,000, a county court bailiff cannot enforce and the judgment has to be transferred up to the High Court if you want it to be enforced by a bailiff attempting to seize goods. The whole case is not transferred up to the High Court, it is a transfer up for the purposes of enforcing by a High Court Enforcement Officer (formerly known as sheriffs).

The right circumstances to use a HCEO are where you have information that the judgment debtor has assets that are easily accessible, i.e. not behind locked doors. For example, if you know the debtor owns an expensive motor car which is parked outside then there is a good prospect of the HCEO being able to make a successful levy on goods.

To transfer a county court judgment up to the High Court for enforcement is a fairly simply process. All that you need to do is to complete an N293A and get that signed by the court and then send that with a copy of the judgment and the court fee of £60 to the HCEO. A N293A is a form on which the county court certifies that there was a judgment entered. A copy of this form is shown in Appendix B.

Alternatively, you can sign and send the instruction form of one of the High Court Enforcement companies and send then the judgment with the court fee and they undertake getting the signed N293A from the court. Which High Court Enforcement company should you instruct? The choice is obviously yours but there are six major players in the market. A factor to consider is the policy of these companies when they collect part payments or instalments from the debtor. Many of the companies will take their fees first from any amount collected and so you may get situations where the HCEO has collected an instalment from the debtor but the creditor will see nothing of it because all the amount collected is swallowed up in the charges of the HCEO.

Some companies will only take a small amount from a collected instalment and so the creditor will actually will receive something from the amount collected. This is something which has influenced my decision to use a company called **High Court Enforcement Group Limited**, whose contact details appear in Appendix A.

Bailiffs/HCEO's have very limited powers of entry. There are very limited situation where force can be used:

- Where bailiff is pursuing an unpaid fine of a criminal nature. The right for bailiffs acting on behalf of the Magistrates Court, the power to "enter and search any premises" for the purpose of executing a Warrant of Distress, was granted under Paragraph 3 of Schedule 4A of the Magistrates Courts Act 2004. This provision was also then inserted into the Domestic Violence, Crime and Victims Act 2004 which was introduced last year. It is important to note that these rules do not apply to the collection of unpaid council tax, business rates, unpaid parking and congestion charge notices, CSA arrears etc. The rules only apply to unpaid fines administered in the Magistrates Court.

- Returning to remove goods that he has seized/taken control of.

Goods cannot be levied upon by simply looking through a window. In the Court of Appeal case of *Evans v South Ribble Borough Council (1991)*, it was decided that in order to levy distress on goods, seize and impound goods, the bailiff must first have gained entry into the premises. In his Judgment, Mr Justice Simon Brown reviewed the law and he concluded the following:

"Once entry is made, very little in the way of seizure and impounding is required......but there must in the first instance be an entry (into the property), thus: it is my clear conclusion that external inspection and posting through the letterbox is a course of action insufficient to bring about the legal consequences of Distress"

Although there are limits on the powers of bailiffs/HCEO's, if the creditor provides plenty of relevant information then there is a much better prospect of seizing the debtor's goods. A HCEO and bailiff have access to DVLA records and so if you know of a vehicle owned by the debtor, then this information (including registration number, vehicle colour and make) should be given on the initial instruction.

A HCEO who is instructed to visit premises which are likely to be open, such as an office open to customers and public houses, provides a better opportunity to seize goods. However, the debtor may then say that all the items on the premises are owned by someone else or are leased. Although the onus is on the debtor to prove that the items are owned by someone else, some HCEO's seem to take the debtor's word for it without the production of conclusive proof. If there is a dispute about ownership, then the matter should be decided by something known as "interpleader proceedings". An example of where interpleader proceedings are used is as follows:

Fred Jones, a HCEO, has a Writ of Fi Fa to execute at the premises of Upton Marble Ltd. Fred attends the premises and seizes a valuable marble stone probably worth several thousand pounds. The judgment debtor claims that the marble is not owned by Upton Marble. The next day, the HCEO receives a contact from Upton Marble (Holdings) Ltd who claim that the stone is their property. The HCEO must notify the judgment creditor immediately and they have seven days in which to say whether the claim by Upton Marble (Holdings) Ltd is admitted or disputed. If the judgment creditor disputes the claim and Upton Marble (Holdings) Ltd does not withdraw their claim, then Fred Jones may issue interpleader proceedings in order for the court to resolve the question of who owns the marble stone.

Once inside a property, a bailiff/HCEO will seize sufficient goods to satisfy the judgment and the costs of enforcement. Often, they will report to the judgment creditor that the value of goods is insufficient to cover the judgment and costs of enforcement. Bailiffs and HCEO's have vast experience of what items would fetch at a sale and so are reluctant to seize goods unless they are certain that the resale value is sufficient. Creditors sometimes feel frustrated when they receive this report but what they do not always realise is that although they may be able to seize a car, for example, the cost of removing it and storing the vehicle until it is sold can be quite costly. Also, the reality is that many second hand goods seized do not fetch much at auction.

There are certain items which a bailiff or HCEO is not permitted to seize:

- Tools, books, vehicles and other items of equipment as are necessary to the debtor for the use by him in his employment, business or vocation
- Clothing bedding, furniture, household equipment and provisions as are necessary for satisfying the basic domestic needs of the debtor and his family

The crucial point is the definition of "necessary". The debtor claiming protection on this basis must give notice to the sheriff within 5 days of the seizure identifying the goods and the grounds for claiming this in respect of each item.

The effectiveness of a bailiff or HCEO can vary. They are restricted by the powers they currently have and the amount of their resources to deal with a heavy workload. It is also useful for the creditor to keep in regular contact with the bailiff or HCEO, and by doing so, their particular case might be dealt with more quickly.

In January 2012, the Government announced that the voluntary code is to be tightened so that people are protected from rogue bailiffs who use unsound, unsafe or unfair methods, while at the same time making sure businesses and authorities can still collect debts fairly. The updated National Standards outline the minimum standards of behaviour expected of bailiffs and bailiff firms, including:

- Bailiffs must not behave in a threatening manner or use unlawful force to gain access to a home or business;

- Bailiffs should avoid discussing the debt with anyone except the person owing money, and bailiffs must never behave in a way that would publicly embarrass a debtor;
- Bailiffs must withdraw when only a child is present; and
- Bailiffs have a duty of care towards vulnerable people, such as the elderly, people with disabilities, single parents and unemployed people and must use discretion when collecting debts from these groups.

Updating the standards is the first step in Government plans to change the way bailiffs are regulated, to make sure they operate fairly for all concerned. The proposals aim to create a new legally-binding regulatory regime for bailiffs. They include:

- New rules around the modes and times of entry to make it clear when and how an enforcement agent may enter a home or a business;
- Which goods are exempt to make it clear which items an enforcement agent may not take from someone's home or business premises; and
- What fees bailiffs can charge for the range of debts that they collect for local government, courts and businesses.

Applying for a charging order

To apply for a charging order it is necessary to:

1. Complete form N379 (if the charge is to be against land, otherwise complete N380)
2. Pay a court fee

In the case of Reeves Printing and Fred Smith, the charge is to be against land and so it is necessary to complete form N379.

The form requires the following information:

- Details of the judgment: when it was entered, at what court and under what claim number
- The full name and address of the judgment debtor
- The amount of the judgment and that which is due at the time of application
- The address of the property or land on which you want to impose a charge
- Information as to whether the judgment debtor owns the property solely or jointly with someone else and evidence to prove it
- Details of any other creditors you know the judgment debtor has, with their names and addresses and the nature of their debt
- Details of any other person who has an interest in the property
- Details of any additional information, apart from the fact that you are owed the money, that you want the court to consider when deciding the application.

The application contains a statement of truth and it has to be signed to confirm that the facts stated are true. If the land is registered, attach the official copy of the land register to prove that the debtor has an interest in the land. Most land in England and Wales is now registered. There are only a few old properties which remain unregistered. Every transaction involving unregistered land will automatically result in the land being registered. Proving the debtor's interest in unregistered land can be more difficult. It would be sensible to attach a witness statement to the charging order application to show the grounds for believing that the debtor has an interest in the unregistered property.

A district judge will consider the application and if satisfied that the debtor has an interest in the property, an interim charging order will be made with a hearing date set to consider whether the order should be made final. The creditor will receive the interim order from the court with sufficient copies to serve on the judgment debtor and any other parties which the courts direct. The interim order and the application must be served not less than 21 days before the hearing on the judgment debtor and any other persons that the court directs. Before you serve the interim order on the debtor, you should register it at the Land Registry so that any person dealing with the land will have notice of the interim charging order and so the property cannot be transacted without the charge being released. This is done by completing the appropriate form and sending it to the Land Registry together with the interim charging order received from the court.

The form can be obtained from the Land Registry website. There is a fee of £50 but this expense should be awarded by the court on making a final charging order. The Land Registry should be notified if the charging order is dismissed.

Applying for an order for sale

The charging order by itself does not produce payment to the creditor. Once a final charging order has been obtained, it is necessary to apply for an order for sale if the creditor wants to realise his money from the proceeds of sale. To apply for an order for sale, a separate "Part 8" claim must be started and a court fee is payable. It is called "Part 8" because CPR Part 8 sets out the procedure. The application must contain the written evidence as required under Practice Direction 73.4(3):

See overleaf.

4.3

The written evidence in support of a claim under rule 73.10 must –
(1) identify the charging order and the property sought to be sold;
(2) state the amount in respect of which the charge was imposed and the amount due at the date of issue of the claim;
(3) verify, so far as known, the debtor's title to the property charged;
(4) state, so far as the claimant is able to identify –
(a) the names and addresses of any other creditors who have a prior charge or other security over the property; and
(b) the amount owed to each such creditor; and
(5) give an estimate of the price which would be obtained on sale of the property.
(6) if the claim relates to land, give details of every person who to the best of the claimant's knowledge is in possession of the property; and
(7) if the claim relates to residential property –
(a) state whether –
(i) a land charge of Class F; or
(ii) a notice under section 31(10) of the Family Law Act 1996, or under any provision of an Act which preceded that section,
has been registered; and
(b) if so, state –
(i) on whose behalf the land charge or notice has been registered; and
(ii) that the claimant will serve notice of the claim on that person.

4.4

The claimant must take all reasonable steps to obtain the information required by paragraph 4.3(4) before issuing the claim.

It can sometimes be difficult to obtain the information needed to make the application or indeed to decide if it is worthwhile making such an application. The rules require a creditor to take all reasonable steps. To obtain the amount of security held by a mortgage company with a first charge is not going to be easy as you will often be met with the reply that we cannot give out that information. If you are not able to establish the amount on a prior charge, it is difficult to know for sure whether there is sufficient equity in the property to make the application worthwhile.

It will also be necessary to obtain an estimate of the price likely to be obtained on sale of the property. Obtaining an accurate valuation may not that easy. A local estate agent may be able to give you an estimate of the property's value but without access to the premises the value is not going to be too precise. An idea of the likely sale price can be obtained by searching property websites but it should be remembered that not knowing if there is sufficient equity in the property is a good reason not to make the application. You do not want to be taking possession of the property to sell it only to find out that there is insufficient equity. It would be sensible to instruct a solicitor to undertake the application for an order for sale as the matter can become complex.

Third Party Debt Order

A third party debt order is an order which freezes money held by a person or organisation such as a bank, which might otherwise be paid to the defendant against whom you have a judgment. The person or organisation that is holding the money is referred to as the "third party". A third party debtor was previously known as a "garnishee order". A third party debt order is commonly used by a judgment creditor where the debtor has a bank account. It is usual for small businesses to keep copies of cheques they receive from customers. It is still possible to apply for a third party debt order if you don't have the debtor's bank account number, but you must at least have the name of the bank and the branch where the account is held. The money held by the third party, must be held solely for the debtor. You cannot, for example, apply for a third party debt order against a joint bank account unless the judgment debt is against both account holders.

The timing of an application for a third party debt order is crucial. If you are applying for an order against the debtor's bank account, it takes affect on the day it is received by the third party and applies to money in the account on that day. So if you have an idea of when the debtor may receive money into the account, such as from their wages, it would be sensible to time the application so that the order will be received by the bank shortly after the money has gone into the account. Although you can try and select the right time for the application, it is still a very hit and miss affair. The order could be served one day before the account receives £1 million but the order would not be applied to that sum! The judgment creditor is therefore taking a gamble but it is hoped that there will be something in the account to make the application worthwhile.

To apply for a third party debt order, form N349 must be completed and sent to the court with the appropriate court fee. The information required on form N349 is:

- The judgment debtor's name and address
- The total amount of the judgment debt and the amount still owing

- The name and address of the third party which must be in England and Wales
- The Head Office of the bank or building society. If known, you should give the name of the branch where the account is held, the branch address, the bank's sort code and the debtor's account number
- Whether or not you know of anyone else who has an interest in the same money
- Whether or not you have made any other applications for a third party debt order in respect of the same judgment
- The reason for your belief that the third party is indebted to the judgment debtor

The last point is probably the most important one. If a business has a copy of a cheque received from the debtor in respect of a previous payment, then the judgment creditor can state this as the reason for their belief and attach a copy of the cheque to the application.

If you want to serve the order yourself then you must tell the court when you send the application, otherwise the court will send it to the third party and judgment debtor. The creditor may wish to serve the order because it gives them control over the best time for the third party to receive it.

The application will be considered by a district judge and if satisfied with the information provided, he will make an interim third party debt order. The interim order will be sent to the third party and 7 days later will be served on the judgment debtor. This is to ensure that the third party freezes the money before the debtor becomes aware of the order. The interim order gives a date for a hearing when the district judge considers whether or not to make the order final. If the order is made final, the third party will have to pay the money to the creditor If the third party is a bank or building society, on receipt of the interim order they are required to carry out a search within 7 days to identify all accounts held by the judgment debtor. They must inform the court and the creditor of the account numbers, whether the account is in credit and if it is they must say whether there is sufficient money to cover the amount being claimed in the interim order.

It is important to remember that trying to attach money due from a bank to a debtor is not the only use of a third party debt order. If the judgment debtor is owed money by its customers, you could apply for a third party debt order against that third party customer. The obvious difficulty here is that the judgment debtor may not give you sufficient or correct information to enable you to state in the application the reason why you believe the third party owes the judgment debtor the money. The Government announced a consultation to improve third party debt orders. The Government's impact assessment of 29 March 2011 states:

"The main policy objectives of the proposed reforms to Third Party Debt Orders (TPDOs) are to streamline and improve the efficiency of the processes, and to make it easier for creditors to enforce their debt through TPDOs. Creditors will be able to apply for TPDOs on a wider range of bank accounts and courts will be able to trace debtors' accounts when they are moved. This should lead to quicker and potentially more successful payment of the judgment debt, and greater confidence in the civil justice system. The proposals should retain safeguards from the aggressive pursuit of debts for debtors complying with judgment orders."

Attachment of Earnings

Where a judgment debtor is employed and has no other substantial assets, then the most effective method of enforcement may be obtaining an attachment of earnings order. The words "may be" should be emphasized as experience suggests that it can be a long winded and bureaucratic method of enforcement. The procedure set out below does not apply if the judgment debtor is a member of the Armed Services. In this instance, the judgment creditor should contact the Ministry of Defence giving details of the outstanding judgment.

An attachment of earning order may be made in respect of wages, salary, fees, bonuses, commission and overtime payable under a contract of employment, including occupational pensions and statutory sick pay. An order cannot be made in respect of self-employed income, nor State pensions and benefits.

Before making the application, it is worth submitting a request for a search of the attachment of earnings index. This can be done by completing form N336 and sending it to the court in the defendant's home area. There is no fee for doing this. The index is a list of all the attachment of earnings orders against people living in that area, including those made by magistrates' courts. If there is already another attachment of earnings order against the defendant, you can ask the court to join your debt with those the debtor already owes. You can get an attachment of earnings order in this way without having to pay a fee.

An application for attachment of earnings order is made by completing form N337 and sending the court fee. An application cannot be made unless the amount of the debt is as least £50. The application must be made to the court in whose district the debtor resides. If the judgment was entered in a court which is not the home court for the debtor, then the case will need to be transferred and this can be done by a letter to the court. The court notifies the debtor of a hearing date at least 21 days in advance, enclosing a questionnaire which must be completed by the debtor and filed at court within eight days of receiving it. If the debtor fails to return the questionnaire which gives a statement of his means, the court may order that it be served personally on the debtor together with a notice warning that if he fails to comply, a committal order may be issued against him.

A copy of the questionnaire is sent to the judgment creditor. The questionnaire is then considered by an administrative officer of the court who may make an attachment of earnings order if there is sufficient information. The officer will take into account how much the judgment debtor needs for food, rent and other essential bills such as electricity. This is called the "protected earnings rate". If the debtor earns more than the protected earnings rate, an order will be made. If either the creditor or the debtor objects, or the court officer decides not to make an order, the application is referred to a district judge for a decision. The order is then sent to the debtor's employer saying how much to take and when to take it. The Centralised Attachment of Earnings System (CAPS) in Northampton is responsible for collecting the payments. Experience suggests that it can take a long period of time to receive payment from CAPS.

A debtor can ask the court for the attachment of earning order to be suspended so that it is not served on his employer. If the court agrees, it will order the debtor to make regular payments direct to the creditor. If the debtor stops paying a suspended order then you can use form N446 to request that the court send the order to the employer. If a debtor becomes unemployed, the order will lapse. However, if he finds new work, the creditor can again request a re-issue of the order to his new employer using N446. There is no fee to request a re-issue of the procedure using form N446.

On the 29 March 2011, the Government announced proposed reforms to attachment of earnings orders. It proposed introducing fixed tables for the calculation for earnings deductions, in place of the current case by case calculations. The powers to make this change are contained in section 91 of the Tribunal, Courts &

Enforcement Act 2007 but this section has not yet been implemented. In addition, there is the intention to introduce the ability for courts, where Attachment of Earnings Orders have failed (due to a change in employment) to request HMCR to provide the name and address of the debtor's current employer for the purposes of re-directing the Order. The power to do this is contained in section 92 of the Tribunal, Courts and Enforcement Act 2007 but it is awaiting implementation.

An order to attend questioning

Orders to attend questioning are likely to be replaced by "Applications for Information Requests" under the TCE Act. The current procedure for obtaining information is set out below followed by the new proposals. An order to attend is basically the old style oral examination with a few modifications. The procedure is very useful if you do not have much information about the finances of the debtor. The creditor can request an individual debtor or a director of the company against whom there is a judgment, to attend court and answer questions. The form also requires the debtor to bring to court papers, such as bank statements and pay slips, as proof. Careful questioning of the debtor can reveal important information to assist in deciding how to enforce the judgment.

To apply for an order, the creditor needs to complete form N316 and send it to the court with the appropriate court fee. The form allows the creditor to add additional questions for the debtor to answer at the hearing. This is important if the creditor or his representative does not intend being at the hearing to question the debtor. If the creditor or his solicitor does not attend, the questioning of the debtor will be conducted by an experienced officer of the court. If the debtor does not reside in the district where the judgment was entered, the court will arrange a hearing date at the debtor's home court. The order to attend questioning has to be served personally on the debtor not less than 14 days before the hearing. If the creditor does not have a solicitor acting, then it will be served by the court bailiff. If the creditor has a solicitor acting, then it is up to the creditor to arrange personal service. In this case, the solicitor will usually instruct a process server to serve the order on the debtor. If it has not been possible to serve the debtor with the order, the judgment creditor must inform the court not less than 7 days before the hearing. If requested, the court will issue a new date for the hearing.

The debtor is entitled to request reasonable travel expenses to attend the hearing. The judgment creditor must either file at court 2 days before the hearing or produce at the hearing, an affidavit which states that:

- Either the debtor has not requested payment of travelling expenses or
- The judgment creditor has paid a sum in accordance with such a request and
- How much of the judgment debt remains unpaid

An affidavit by the person who served the order (unless it was the court bailiff) giving details of how and when it was served also needs to be filed or produced at the court hearing.

If you can show a good reason, you can request that the questioning take place before a district judge. However, the district judge will consider whether or not the reason given justifies questioning being undertaken before a judge instead of an officer of the court. The problem with orders to attend questioning is that the dates being set are usually many months ahead because of the busy court lists. Also, if you have a solicitor acting, then you will incur the cost of instructing a process server to serve the order.

There has been one improvement over the old oral examination. If the debtor fails to show up at the hearing after being served with the order or refuses to answer questions at the hearing, then a judge can issue a committal order. Under the old system of oral examinations, the order was initially served on the debtor by post. If he did not attend the hearing then another date would have been set and the notice served personally by the court bailiff. If they did not attend the second hearing, then a committal could be made. So with the new procedure, if a debtor does not attend then the court can move to a committal order more quickly. The threat of a committal to prison gives an order to attend some teeth but in some situations it may be difficult for the court bailiff to serve a committal order or to make an arrest.

Enforcement conclusions

There are often unrealistic expectations on the part of creditors as to the actual amount of money they are likely to collect from debtors. It is important for creditors to consider the appropriate method of enforcing a judgment debt. In many situations, especially where the judgment debtor is a consumer, sending in bailiffs/enforcement officers may well have limited effect. High Court Enforcement Officers may well have a good prospect of success if the judgment debtor is a business, for example it is trading from a public house where there is a good chance of gaining entry or the debtor is a car dealer and there are many cars on an open forecourt. In my experience, if a debtor has an interest in a property which has equity, then there is a good prospect of recovering a debt. However, if the minimum limits below which courts will not grant charging orders are introduced, then the prospects of enforcing smaller debts will become more difficult. If creditors retain better information about their customers, such as recording bank details, then third party debt orders become a possible way of enforcing a judgment.

Chapter 7

Insolvency and Bankruptcy

Insolvency or bankruptcy is a rather drastic method of attempting to obtain money awarded on a judgment. The option is available where the creditor is owed more than £750. The company should be given 21 days notice to settle the debt in the form of a statutory demand. If there is no dispute about the debt, a statutory demand can be issued without having obtained a court judgment. However, there have been a number of cases in the Court of Appeal warning creditors that bankruptcy and insolvency should not be used as a debt collection tool. If there are issues, then the creditor should obtain a judgment first and then start bankruptcy or winding up proceedings. If a statutory demand is issued where there is a dispute, the debtor can apply to set aside the statutory demand and the court is likely to penalise the creditor by awarding costs to the debtor.

If a statutory demand is not settled, then a bankruptcy or winding up petition can be presented to the court. There is a court fee to present a petition as well as the requirement to pay a deposit to the Official Receiver when presenting a winding up petition and for a bankruptcy petition. The fees have increased quite significantly in recent years.

If a company is wound up by the court, the liquidator is the Official Receiver who is a government employee. If the company has assets the Official Receiver calls for a creditors meeting at which an Insolvency Practitioner is appointed liquidator, to realise the assets and then distribute the proceeds to the creditors. If an individual is made bankrupt, then a trustee in bankruptcy is appointed.

The Enterprise Act 2002 has made some significant changes to insolvency and bankruptcy. Some of the main provisions of the Act include streamlining the procedure for administration orders in respect of companies and to restrict the ability of lenders to appoint administrative receivers. In the area of bankruptcy, the number of restrictions automatically imposed on un-discharged bankrupts has been reduced and provides for the discharge of nearly all bankrupts after 12 months. In certain circumstances, there can be an early release from bankruptcy, even earlier than 12 months. The Enterprise Act 2002 also removed Crown Preference, which had given the Crown preferential rights in all insolvencies.

What are the main consequences of bankruptcy?

On the making of a bankruptcy order, the Official Receiver or trustee in bankruptcy will have control over all of the debtor's assets and finances. The bankrupt must co-operate fully with the Official Receiver. The Official Receiver will tell creditors that you are bankrupt. Any legal action commenced before the bankruptcy order will be stayed and creditors will be prevented from taking any further action against the debtor for debts incurred before the bankruptcy order. The Official Receiver may act as the trustee or may arrange a meeting of creditors for them to choose an insolvency practitioner to be the trustee. This happens if it appears there are significant assets. If the debtor has a home, then that may be sold to go towards paying creditors.

The trustee will tell the creditors how much money will be shared out in the bankruptcy. Creditors then have to make their formal claims. The costs of the bankruptcy proceedings are paid first from the money that is available. The costs include fees that the Official Receiver or the insolvency practitioner charges for administering the bankruptcy. If the Official Receiver's investigation reveals dishonesty or that the bankrupt was at all to blame for his financial position, the Official Receiver may apply for a "bankruptcy restrictions order" which may extend the period of the bankruptcy.

An un-discharged bankrupt must not:

- obtain credit of £500 or more either alone or jointly with another person without disclosing your bankruptcy. This is not just borrowing money - it includes you getting credit as a result of a statement or conduct which is designed to get credit, even though you have not made a specific agreement for it. For example, ordering goods without asking for credit and then failing to pay for them when they are delivered);

- carry on business (directly or indirectly) in a different name from that which he/she was made bankrupt, without telling all those with whom you do business the name in which you were made bankrupt;

- directly or indirectly be concerned in the promoting, forming or managing of a limited company, or acting as a company director without the court's permission, whether formally appointed as a director or not

Voluntary arrangements

Other recent legislation, such as the Insolvency Act 2000, has made it easier for companies and individuals to make use of voluntary arrangements. A voluntary arrangement is where a company or individual enters into an agreement with creditors. An approved voluntary arrangement means that creditors are bound by its terms and so cannot take action in respect of debts arising before the date of the arrangement. The Insolvency Act introduced provisions which make it possible for a creditor to be bound by a voluntary arrangement even if they did not receive notice of the meeting at which the proposal was voted upon. The new procedure introduced by the legislation is open to abuse by rogue directors and individuals. It again emphasizes the importance of checking out the finances of a potential new customer before doing business with them, as it is easier for debtors to avoid payment.

Debt Relief Orders

A Debt Relief Order (DRO) is a quick and cheap alternative to bankruptcy for those who have no assets and little income. To be eligible for a DRO, the total amount of debt must be less than £15,000; assets must be worth under £300 and a disposable income of less then £50 per month. The Official Receiver will then carry out certain checks to verify information provided. Applicants will be allowed to have a vehicle with a value of less than £1,000.

DRO's are not available through the court system. Instead, the orders will be made by an Official Receiver, and there is a separate unit for this purpose at the Official Receiver's office in Plymouth. An application for a DRO will be made online, through an authorized intermediary. There is a fee to apply for a DRO which covers the cost of the administration. Once the order is made, creditors who are included in the DRO will then be prevented from taking any action to recover or enforce their debts against the debtor. The restrictions of a DRO are similar to that of bankruptcy, for example obtaining credit above £500 without declaring the DRO and not being permitted to be involved in the formation or management of a company.

The debts will be discharged at the end of one year. If the finances of the debtor improve, then they would be expected to make arrangement to repay their creditors. The Official Receiver has powers of enquiry and enforcement and so if a creditor advises the Official Receiver of substantial assets or liabilities not disclosed in the DRO application, then the Official Receive may investigate.

Chapter 8

What changes are needed to commercial debt recovery?

There is a need to provide businesses with a faster method of collecting debts. For whatever reason, the county courts are not providing an efficient process for the recovery of unpaid accounts. This chapter suggests a streamlined legal procedure for "business to business" debt recovery.

There needs to be a balance between a system that allows for the speedy recovery of debt but builds in safeguards that avoids abuse by allowing genuine disputes to be raised. The current county court process takes too long to arrive at a position where you can enforce a judgment. The reasons for this may include too many cases and insufficient resources. If that is the case, then there is a strong argument for a process where the creditor does most of the administrative work such as the service and production of documents. Also, if the matter reached a point where a decision is required, the creditor books a venue, and when that is done, the court provides details of the judge to hear the case.

This could be achieved with a new procedure along the lines set out below. A new dedicated court could be established to handle commercial debt recovery. In the same way that a new CCMCC has been established in Salford, a "Commercial Debt Recovery Centre" could be set up.

PROPOSED NEW PROCEDURE FOR COMMERCIAL DEBT RECOVERY:

1. When a business is owed money by another business, before court action can be commenced, the creditor must send a formal Demand Notice. The letter of demand would be in a specified form, although at this stage a court action would not be formally started, as in the case of a statutory demand. The formal Demand Notice would give the debtor 21 days from the date of service in which to pay or file a formal Notice of Reply.

DEMAND NOTICE

This Demand Notice is served by: ***Fred Smith Ltd*** *(business creditor)*

Address: ***10 Church Lane, Newtown, NW12 2BT***

Tel. 01234 568 123 Fax. 01234 579 800

On you the business debtor: ***Bloggs Ltd***

Of: 2 Water Lane, Newtown, NB 13 5YU

TAKE NOTICE THAT UNLESS YOU SETTLE THIS DEBT TO THE SATISFACTION OF THE BUSINESS CREDITOR WITHIN 21 CALENDER DAYS OF THE DATE THIS DEMAND IS SERVED ON YOU, THE BUSINESS CREDITOR CAN APPLY TO THE COURT FOR COURT JUDGMENT AGAINST YOU.

Amount Claimed: £6,000

Details of the debt:

The Creditor supplied computer software to the Debtor on

the xx/xx/xx. The software was a time management system. The software was installed on the debtor's computer network and the creditor has not been notified of any problems. The Creditor invoiced the Debtor and as per the terms of business the debtor had 30 days to pay the invoice. A copy of the invoice is attached to this Demand Notice. The invoice became due on 1 July 20xx and it remains unpaid. The Creditor claim interest from the date the invoice became due until the date the date of this demand and continuing at a daily rate of £______. Attached to this demand are the terms of business that applied to this contract.

Sworn by M Smith) M Smith

Managing Director)

Fred Smith Ltd)

On the 1st day of December 20xx

Before me: A R Jones

Commissioner for Oaths

To ensure that the Demand Notice is received by the debtor, it would have to be personally served on the Debtor at the business address of the debtor.

2. If the Debtor does not pay or serve a Notice of Reply within 21 calendar days, then the creditor can apply to the county court for a Judgment in default of a Demand Notice. The application to the court requires the completion of a request for Judgment form and the payment of a court fee. With the Request, the creditor has to file an affidavit of service to prove service of the demand and confirm

that there has been no payment or Notice of Reply received. The request form would need to be sworn by the creditor to confirm the outstanding amount and that no Notice of Reply has been received. The court will then issue to the creditor a judgment and this has to be served on the debtor personally. The creditor has to file at the court an affidavit of service. Upon service of the Judgment in default, the debtor can apply to set it aside if it can show that it has a good reason why it did not respond to the Demand Notice and that it has a genuine defence to the claim.

3. If the Debtor responds to the Demand Notice disputing the claim by the creditor, then the court will then ask the parties to state any dates when they are not available for a hearing, the likely number of witnesses, and probable length of the hearing. The court then sends out a "trial window" and the time estimate for the hearing and it is for the creditor to fix a hearing date within that trial window and find a venue for the trial in the creditor's home town/ city or nearest town or city. When the creditor has booked a venue and date, it notifies the court and debtor. The court then sends out the name of the district judge/adjudicator who will hear the case and an invoice for the Judge's fee which must be paid within 10 days.

Summary of procedure

1. Creditor sends Demand Notice to Debtor

2. Within 21 days, the debtor files a response to the Demand Notice

3. The court requests available dates from both parties.

4. Court sends out trial window for the creditor to book a hearing date and venue within the trial window. The earliest date in the trial window will be 6 weeks ahead.

5. The creditor must book a date and venue for hearing within 10 days and provide the court and the debtor the date and place of the hearing.

6. The court will then send out the name of the district judge for the hearing and the creditor must pay the hearing fee within 10 days of receiving the notice

The advantage of the proposed procedure for commercial debt recovery is that it takes away a lot of the involvement by the court offices and thus has the potential for being a speedier method of deciding a defended case. The serving of documents and arranging of a venue which is not a court building will hopefully mean that businesses are not waiting on the courts to plod through the administration. It would probably be more expensive but it may be a price worth paying if it means a quick decision.

Not only do we need to change the processes leading up to a decision, but we need to make it simpler to enforce what you are awarded. Not only do we want enforcement procedures with teeth, but a streamlining of the processes themselves. The ordinary person will often think once they have got their judgment from the court that all they need to do is wave the Judgment under the debtor's nose and that document has the power to make the debtor pay up. It often comes as a surprise that the Judgment does not convey the power to force the money to be handed over by the debtor. Instead, they have to go through further procedures and pay more court fees so that some more paper is created telling the debtor to pay. Why not adapt the Judgment itself so that it contains a general power so that when served on a third party, e.g. a bank, they must pay over any money held to the value of the Judgment. This would cut out some of the administration involved for example in applying for a third party debt order. The same type of logic has often been expressed in the setting of possession proceedings. Once a possession order is obtained, clients often wonder why it is then necessary to pay another court fee so that a warrant to evict the tenant is issued to the bailiff to evict the tenant. Why not make provision so that once the date for the possession has passed, the landlord can simply recover possession. There would need to be safeguards but it is surely not beyond the imagination of lawyers.

Chapter 9

Insolvency, Administration and the Personal Liability of Directors

The severe economic downturn in the UK economy in late 2008 and through into 2009, lead to some major high street names going into Administration and ultimately going under. There has been much suspicion about the motives in some cases when a company is put into administration. Unsecured creditors, quite rightly in some instances, suspect that there may be wrong-doing when a company is put into administration by the directors, as a means to dispose of debts. This chapter examines what small businesses and credit managers need to know about liquidation, administration and what they can do to recover unpaid account and the prospects of holding directors personally liable.

Personal liability of directors

Although the general rule is that directors of a limited company, or the partners of a limited liability partnership, are not personally responsible for the company's debts, there are circumstances when the director can be made to contribute to the debts of the company. There are cases where courts have been prepared to lift the veil of incorporation if there is evidence that the limited company was merely a "sham". This principle stems from a case of ***Gilford Motor Co v Horne [1933]*** where an individual bound by a non-solicitation covenant after the termination of his employment set up in business through a limited company. The individual was held to be in breach of covenant, despite the formation of the company, because the company was formed as a device to effectively carrying on a business of the individual. A more recent case ***Trustor v Smallbone (2001)*** expressed the view that a court should pierce the corporate veil if the company was used as a device or façade to conceal the true facts thereby avoiding or concealing any liability of individuals.

The courts are reluctant to lift the veil of incorporation and so do not expect this argument to be accepted by district judges unless there is convincing evidence that there was deceit on the part of the directors. However the case of ***Contex Drouzhba Ltd v Wiseman (2007)***, provides another situation where a director can be personally liable. Lord Justice Waller in the Court of Appeal summarized the case as follows:

Section 6 of Lord Tenterden's Act (the Statute of Frauds (Amendment) Act 1828) states:-

"Action not maintainable on representations of character etc, unless they be in writing signed by the Party chargeable."

No action shall be brought whereby to charge any person upon or by reason of any representation or assurance made or given concerning or relating to the character, conduct, credit, ability, trade, or dealings of any other person to the intent or purpose that such other person may obtain credit, money, or goods upon, unless such representation or assurance be made in writing, signed by the Party to be charged therewith."

By a judgment handed down on 3rd November 2006, Irwin J found that Mr Wiseman as a director of Scott Daniel Limited (SD) signed a document dated 9th January 1998 containing a promise by the company to pay for goods to be ordered in the future. He found that Mr Wiseman in so doing impliedly represented that the company had the capacity to meet its obligations to pay for goods to be ordered thereafter. He found that that representation was made fraudulently by Mr Wiseman who he held knew the company did not have that capacity and had no chance of gaining it. On that basis he found that Mr Wiseman was liable in damages for deceit. He found critically so far as this appeal is concerned that the representation was "made in writing, signed by the party to be charged [Mr Wiseman]" and that thus the above section of Lord Tenterden's Act provided no defence.

The decision of the Judge at first instance was appealed. The Court of Appeal held:

- where the director was effectively the mind of the company, as Wiseman was, and where he signed a document on behalf of the company containing a representation he knew to be fraudulent, it was clear that the director could be personally liable for his own fraud

- in this case, Wiseman had impliedly represented that the company had the capacity to pay. Wiseman had known this to be untrue and the judge had been entitled to hold that Wiseman had made a fraudulent representation in writing, and was therefore the 'person to be charged' within section 6

- whilst the Act required the representation to be in writing there was no reason why the director's signature on the document would not be sufficient evidence to show a representation was made in writing by the person charged so that the section 6 defence did not apply.

The case raises a number of questions. Much depends on whether the courts are prepared to apply the principle of director's personal liability in deceit to factual situations that differ materially from the circumstances in the Contex case. Whilst most of the appeal was concerned with the section 6 defence, the case is more important for what it says about the potential liability of directors who sign agreements on behalf of their company. Athough each case will depend on its own facts, there is a good chance that if a director (who is the controlling mind of the company) makes a fraudulent representation that the company can make payment by signing a contract on behalf of the company, he will be personally liable in deceit. Therefore, the implications of this case are very important.

A situation which may give rise to personal liability against a company director is where a new company is started with a similar name to the one that has gone insolvent and the director of the new company was also a director of the old company in the 12 months prior to it going into liquidation. In short, the Insolvency Act 1986 it makes it an offence for a director of a company that has gone into insolvent liquidation to be a director of another company that is known by a similar name and there may be personal liability on that director for the debts of the successor company.

This scenario is commonly known as "the phoenix rising from the ashes". Suppose, for example, you were a director of a company called Fred Bloggs Ltd and it goes into insolvent liquidation. If you start up new company called "Fred Bloggs 2007 Ltd" of which you are a director, then you could be in breach of the legislation. If Fred Bloggs 2007 Ltd incurs debts then you could be personally liable for the debts of the company. There are circumstances where this would not apply where:

- the director obtains leave of the court

- the business is bought by the successor company under arrangements made by the Insolvency Practitioner and the required notice has been given to creditors

- where the successor company has been known by the name in question for 12 months before the liquidation and has not been dormant during that period.

Fraudulent and wrongful trading[4] as well as trading while insolvent may mean that a director has to contribute personally to the debts of the company. The Liquidator has a duty to consider the conduct of the directors prior to the insolvency and if there is evidence of wrongful trading or fraudulent trading, their report to the Secretary of State may recommend that action be taken. However, the Liquidator may require the creditors to contribute towards the cost of taking action against the director. If the directors are found to have engaged in wrongful or fraudulent trading, then the directors can be ordered to make a personal contribution to the debts of the company. A personal contribution from the directors increases the amount available to distribute among creditors. In reality, there are not many prosecutions against directors for breaches of company law, due to the limited resources of those investigating the activities of directors.

In view of the fact that Liquidators are unlikely to make applications for directors to contribute personally towards the debts of a company, I believe that there needs to be amendments to the Insolvency Act 1986. To permit creditors to make an application against a director for fraudulent and wrongful trading would require a minor amendment to the Act as suggested below:

Proposed Insolvency Amendment Bill

A Bill to amend the Insolvency Act 1986 that will permit creditors of an insolvent company to apply to court under section 213 and section 214 of the Insolvency Act 1986.

4 sections 213 and 214 of the Insolvency Act 1986

1. *In section 213 (2) of the Insolvency Act 1986, after the word "liquidator" insert the words "or a creditor of the company".*
2. *In section 214 (1) of the Insolvency Act 1986, after the word "liquidator" insert the words "or a creditor of the company"*

The simple 2 clause amendment Bill would mean that sections 213 and 214 would read as follows after amendments. The proposed amendments are in bold.

Insolvency Act 1986

213.
Fraudulent trading.

— (1) If in the course of the winding up of a company it appears that any business of the company has been carried on with intent to defraud creditors of the company or creditors of any other person, or for any fraudulent purpose, the following has effect.

(2) The court, on the application of the liquidator ***or a creditor of the company*** *may declare that any persons who were knowingly parties to the carrying on of the business in the manner above-mentioned are to be liable to make such contributions (if any) to the company's assets as the court thinks proper.*

214.
Wrongful trading.

— (1) Subject to subsection (3) below, if in the course of the winding up of a company it appears that subsection (2) of this section applies in relation to a person who is or has been a director

of the company, the court, on the application of the liquidator ***or a creditor of the company****, may declare that that person is to be liable to make such contribution (if any) to the company's assets as the court thinks proper.*

(2) This subsection applies in relation to a person if—

(a) the company has gone into insolvent liquidation,

(b) at some time before the commencement of the winding up of the company, that person knew or ought to have concluded that there was no reasonable prospect that the company would avoid going into insolvent liquidation, and

(c) that person was a director of the company at that time;

Administration

Administration is when a person, 'the administrator', is appointed to manage a company's affairs, business and property for the benefit of the creditors. The person appointed must be an insolvency practitioner and has the status of an officer of the court (whether or not he or she is appointed by the court).

The main objectives of administration are to:

- rescue a company as a going concern;
- achieve a better price for the company's assets or otherwise realise their value more favourably for the creditors as a whole than would be likely if the company were wound up (without first being in administration); or

- in certain circumstances, realise the value of property in order to make a distribution to one or more preferential creditors.

A company enters administration when the appointment of an administrator takes effect. An administrator may be appointed by:

- an administration order made by the court;
- the holder of a floating charge; or
- the company or its directors.

When a company enters administration any pending winding-up petitions will be dismissed or suspended and there will be a moratorium on insolvency and on other legal proceedings.

As soon as reasonably practicable, an administrator must send a notice of his or her appointment to the company and each of its creditors and publish notice of his or her appointment in the Gazette and in a newspaper in the area where the company has its principal place of business.

In recent times there has been much attention given to "Pre-Pack Administrations". This is the sale by a company administrator of assets immediately on (or at least very soon after) being appointed, which has been arranged prior to the administrator's appointment. Creditors of a company in administration often blame the management of the company for their predicament. Through the use of the pre-packaged administration, the management, or somebody with close links to the management, can often buy the assets of the company at a greatly reduced price and free of debts. This has rightly caused some creditors to raise concerns about some administrations.

As a result of these concerns, a new Statement of Insolvency Practice 16 (SIP 16)) has been introduced. SIP 16 includes guidance on disclosure:

> *8. It is in the nature of a pre-packaged sale in an administration that unsecured creditors are not given the opportunity to consider the sale of the business or assets before it takes place. It is important, therefore, that they are provided with a detailed explanation and justification of why a pre-packaged sale was undertaken, so that they can be satisfied that the administrator has acted with due regard for their interests.*
>
> *9. The following information should be disclosed to creditors in all cases where there is a pre-packaged sale, as far as the administrator is aware after making appropriate enquiries:*
>
> - *The source of the administrator's initial introduction*
> - *The extent of the administrator's involvement prior to appointment*
> - *Any marketing activities conducted by the company and/or the administrator*
> - *Any valuations obtained of the business or the underlying assets*
> - *The alternative courses of action that were considered by the administrator, with an explanation of possible financial outcomes*
> - *Why it was not appropriate to trade the business, and offer it for sale as a going concern, during the administration*
> - *Details of requests made to potential funders to fund working capital requirements*
> - *Whether efforts were made to consult with major creditors*

- *The date of the transaction*
- *Details of the assets involved and the nature of the transaction*
- *The consideration for the transaction, terms of payment, and any condition of the contract that could materially affect the consideration*
- *If the sale is part of a wider transaction, a description of the other aspects of the transaction*
- *The identity of the purchaser*
- *Any connection between the purchaser and the directors, shareholders or secured creditors of the company*
- *The names of any directors, or former directors, of the company who are involved in the management or ownership of the purchaser, or of any other entity into which any of the assets are transferred*
- *Whether any directors had given guarantees for amounts due from the company to a prior financier, and whether that financier is financing the new business*
- *Any options, buy-back arrangements or similar conditions attached to the contract of sale*

In January 2012, the Government announced that there would be no change to the pre-pack regime. However, in May 2012, the business minster, Norman Lamb chaired a meeting to review the current controls on pre-packs. It is not known whether there will be any changes in the short term to the rules concerning pre-packs, but it continues to be a controversial procedure. In 2011, the Insolvency Service received information on 723 pre-pack cases, 419 of these were reviewed with a finding that 32% of these were not fully compliant with the disclosure requirements under SIP 16.[5] So the view remains among many credit managers that pre-packs are a way of avoiding paying your creditors.

[5] Credit Today Magazine, June 2012.

Although section 212 of the Insolvency Act 1986 (see the end of the chapter) does provide a mechanism to challenge activities of an administrator, the creditor is likely to have to find a considerable amount in legal fees to make the application and even if successful it may only mean a director administrator contributing to a fund available to pay all creditors and not just the creditor who made the application. Obviously a group of creditors may wish to join together to take action, in reality the "rogue director" will be relying on the fact that creditors will not want to spend too much money investigating the circumstances of the administration and will be able to buy the assets of the company at a knock down price and clear off a load of debts.

INSOLVENCY ACT 1986
Penalisation of directors and officers

Section 212. Summary remedy against delinquent directors, liquidators, etc.

(1) This section applies if in the course of the winding up of a company it appears that a person who -

(a) is or has been an officer of the company,

(b) has acted as liquidator, administrator or administrative receiver of the company, or

(c) not being a person falling within paragraph (a) or (b), is or has been concerned, or has taken part, in the promotion, formation or management of the company,

has misapplied or retained, or become accountable for, any money or other property of the company, or been guilty of any misfeasance or breach of any fiduciary or other duty in relation to the company.

(2) The reference in subsection (1) to any misfeasance or breach of any fiduciary or other duty in relation to the company includes, in the case of a person who has acted as liquidator or administrator of the company, any misfeasance or breach of any fiduciary or other duty in connection with the carrying out of his functions as liquidator or administrator of the company.

(3) The court may, on the application of the official receiver or the liquidator, or of any creditor or contributory, examine into the conduct of the person falling within subsection (1) and compel him -

(a) to repay, restore or account for the money or property or any part of it, with interest at such rate as the court thinks just, or

(b) to contribute such sum to the company's assets by way of compensation in respect of the misfeasance or breach of fiduciary or other duty as the court thinks just.

(4) The power to make an application under subsection (3) in relation to a person who has acted as liquidator or administrator of the company is not exercisable, except with the leave of the court, after that person has had his release.

(5) The power of a contributory to make an application under subsection (3) is not exercisable except with the leave of the court, but is exercisable notwithstanding that he will not benefit from any order the court may make on the application.

Appendix A

Useful Sources of Information

The internet has become a valuable source of information. The following is a list of useful web sites that provide information on debt recovery and legal issues.

- The Ministry of Justice

www.justice.gov.uk

This was the Department for Constitutional Affairs before it was renamed. It provides the latest court rules and consultations papers where there are proposed to change the law.

- The Court Service

www.hmcourts-service.gov.uk

This is a useful site as it provides all the court forms which can be downloaded as well as the current level of court fees, recent court judgments and the addresses of every county court in England and Wales.

- The Better Payment Practice Campaign

www.payontime.co.uk

This site promotes good payment practices amongst UK businesses. It provides information on the Late Payment legislation.

- Credit Today Magazine

www.credittoday.co.uk

Credit Today is a monthly magazine which considers all aspects of debt recovery and credit control.

Other addresses:

- The Institute of Credit Management

The ICM is the professional body representing the interests of people in all sectors of credit management. www.icm.org.uk

- British and Irish Legal Information Institute

This site provides free access to British and Irish Legal Information, including law reports. www.bailii.org

- First Report

First Report provides instant access to quality credit reports on any UK company that tell you exactly what you need to know to make credit decisions quickly and easily. www.firstreport.co.uk

- Companies House

All limited companies in England, Wales and Scotland are registered at Companies House, an Executive Agency of the Department for Business, Enterprise and Regulatory Reform (BERR). There are more than 2 million limited companies registered in Great Britain, and more than 300,000 new companies are incorporated each year.

www.companieshouse.gov.uk

- Private & Trade Investigations

Tracing and processing serving services.
Contact: Don Smith
Tel: 01373 858411
E-mail: covertowl@aol.com

- The Insolvency Service

Tel. *0845 602 9848* www.insolvency.gov.uk

Index

Appendix B:
A Selection of Court Forms

N1 – Claim Form

N244 – Application Form (application for Summary Judgment)

N149 – Allocation Questionnaire (small claims track)

Claim Form

In the	
Upton County Court	

	for court use only
Claim No.	
Issue date	

Claimant(s) name(s) and address(es) including postcode

Reeves Publishing Ltd
10 Market Place
Upton
UP1 1PA

Defendant(s) name

Mr Fred Smith

Brief details of claim

Debt Action
Claim for the price of goods and services provided

Value

£3,000 plus interest and fixed costs

You must indicate your preferred court for hearings here *(see notes for guidance)*

Upton County Court

endant's
ne and
'ress,
uding
tcode

Mr Fred Smith
18 Victoria Street
Upton
UP2 2PS

	£
Amount claimed	3,073.65
Court fee	120.00
Solicitor's costs	
Total amount	3,193.65

When corresponding with the court, please address forms or letters to the Court Manager and quote the claim number.

Claim No.	

Does, or will, your claim include any issues under the Human Rights Act 1998? ☐ Yes ■ No

Particulars of Claim (attached)(to follow)

1. The Claimant's Claim is the agreed price for printing and binding 1000 copies of the Defendant's novel.
2. The Claimant and Defendant signed a contract dated the 1 June XXXX, a copy of which is attached to these particulars of claim. For the price of £3,000, the Claimant agreed to print and bind 1000 copies of the Defendant's book. The Claimant received the manuscript on disc in Word format from the Defendant on 7 June XXXX. The Claimant printed and bound the paper into a book. The 1000 copies were delivered to the Defendant on the 25 June XXXX and payment in full was due by 21 July XXXX. The Claimant has not received payment of the said sum of £3,000 despite several reminders.
3. The Claimant believes it has complied with Protocols on Pre-Action Conduct.
4. The Claimant claims the said sum of £3,000 and interest according to section 69 of the County Courts Act 1984 at the rate of 8% per annum from the 21 July.

AND THE CLAIMANT CLAIMS:
i. the said sum of £3,000
ii. interest at the rate of 8% from the 21 July to the date of this Claim Form (10 November XXXX) being £73.65 and continuing at a daily rate of £0.65 until judgment or sooner payment

Statement of Truth
*(I believe)(The Claimant believes) that the facts stated in these particulars of claim are true.
* I am duly authorised by the claimant to sign this statement

Full name Brian Reeves

Name of claimant's solicitor's firm ____________________

signed ____________________ position or office held Director

*(Claimant)(Litigation friend)(Claimant's solicitor) (if signing on behalf of firm or company)

**delete as appropriate*

Claimant's or claimant's solicitor's address to which documents or payments should be sent if different from overleaf including (if appropriate) details of DX, fax or e-mail.

Application notice

For help in completing this form please read the notes for guidance form N244Notes.

Name of court	Upton County Court
Claim no.	2UP12200
Warrant no. (if applicable)	
Claimant's name (including ref.)	Reeves Publishing Ltd
Defendant's name (including ref.)	Fred Smith
Date	xx/xx/xx

1. What is your name or, if you are a solicitor, the name of your firm?

2. Are you a ☑ Claimant ☐ Defendant ☐ Solicitor

   ☐ Other *(please specify)*

   If you are a solicitor whom do you represent?

3. What order are you asking the court to make and why?

   We seek summary Judgment under CPR Part 24 because the Defendant has no real prospect of successfully defending this claim and there is no other compelling reason for a trial.

4. Have you attached a draft of the order you are applying for? ☑ Yes ☐ No

5. How do you want to have this application dealt with? ☑ at a hearing ☐ without a hearing ☐ at a telephone hearing

6. How long do you think the hearing will last? Hours 30 Minutes

   Is this time estimate agreed by all parties? ☐ Yes ☑ No

7. Give details of any fixed trial date or period: none

8. What level of Judge does your hearing need? District Judge

9. Who should be served with this application? Defendant

10. What information will you be relying on, in support of your application?

- [ ] the attached witness statement
- [ ] the statement of case
- [x] the evidence set out in the box below

If necessary, please continue on a separate sheet.

The Claimant printed and bound 1000 copies of the Defendant's book. The manuscript was provided by the Defendant and the Claimant did not edit or alter the text. The Claimant chased for payment by letter on several occasions between 21st July XXXX and 20 October XXXX for the amount due but no response was received and no indication that there was any problem with the binding of the books.

In fact, on the 30th September XXXX, I spoke to Fred Smith who said that he was very pleased with the book and would arrange payment by the end of the week. A letter warning of court action was sent on 20th October XXXX but no reply was received and court action was issued. The first the defendant mentioned the allegedly faulty book binding was in the defence. The defendant has still not shown the Claimant any book which he alleges has defective binding.

The respondents attention is drawn to CPR 24 r5.1, where any written evidence to be relied on must be filed at court at least 7 days before the hearing date.

Statement of Truth

(I believe) (The applicant believes) that the facts stated in this section (and any continuation sheets) are true.

Signed ____________________ Dated ____________________

Applicant('s Solicitor)('s litigation friend)

Full name Brian Reeves

Name of applicant's solicitor's firm ____________________

Position or office held Director
(if signing on behalf of firm or company)

---

11. Signature and address details

Signed ____________________ Dated ____________________

Applicant('s Solicitor)('s litigation friend)

Position or office held ____________________
(if signing on behalf of firm or company)

Applicant's address to which documents about this application should be sent

Reeves Publishing Ltd
10 Market Place
Upton

Postcode: UP11 1PA

If applicable	
Phone no.	01213 4445 555
Fax no.	
DX no.	
Ref no.	

E-mail address	

pplication Notice (Form N244) – Notes for Guidance

Court Staff cannot give legal advice. If you need information or advice on a legal problem you can contact Community Legal Service Direct on 0845 345 4 345 or www.clsdirect.org.uk, or a Citizens Advice Bureau. Details of your local offices and contact numbers are available via their website www.citizensadvice.org.uk

aying the court fee
court fee is payable depending on the type of plication you are making. For example:

- To apply for judgment to be set aside
- To apply to vary a judgment or suspend enforcement
- To apply for a summons or order for a witness to attend
- To apply by consent, or without service of the application notice, for a judgment or order.

o fee is payable for an application by consent for an djournment of a hearing if it is received by the court least 14 days before the date of the hearing.

hat if I cannot afford the fee?
you show that a payment of a court fee would volve undue hardship to you, you may be eligible for fee concession.

or further information, or to apply for a fee concession, sk court staff for a copy of the combined booklet and rm EX160A - Court fees - Do I have to pay them? is is also available from any county court office, or a py of the leaflet can be downloaded from our website ww.hmcourts-service.gov.uk

ompleting the form

uestion 3
et out what order you are applying for and why; g. to adjourn the hearing because..., to set aside a dgment against me because... etc.

uestion 5
ost applications will require a hearing and you ll be expected to attend. The court will allocate a earing date and time for the application. Please dicate in a covering letter any dates that you are available within the next six weeks.

e court will only deal with the application 'without a earing' in the following circumstances.

Where all the parties agree to the terms of the order being asked for;

Where all the parties agree that the court should deal with the application without a hearing, or

Where the court does not consider that a hearing would be appropriate.

Telephone hearings are only available in applications where at least one of the parties involved in the case is legally represented. Not all applications will be suitable for a telephone hearing and the court may refuse your request.

Question 6
If you do not know how long the hearing will take do not guess but leave these boxes blank.

Question 7
If your case has already been allocated a hearing date or trial period please insert details of those dates in the box.

Question 8
If your case is being heard in the High Court or a District Registry please indicate whether it is to be dealt with by a Master, District Judge or Judge.

Question 9
Please indicate in the box provided who you want the court to send a copy of the application to.

Question 10
In this section please set out the information you want the court to take account of in support of the application you are making.
If you wish to rely on:

- **a witness statement,** tick the first box and attach the statement to the application notice. A witness statement form is available on request from the court office.
- **a statement of case,** tick the second box if you intend to rely on your particulars of claim or defence in support of your application.
- **written evidence** on this form, tick the third box and enter details in the space provided. You must also complete the statement of truth. Proceedings for contempt of court may be brought against a person who signs a statement of truth without an honest belief in its truth.

Question 11
The application must be signed and include your current address and contact details. If you agree that the court and the other parties may communicate with you by Document Exchange, telephone, facsimile or email, complete the details

Before returning your form to the court

Have you:

- signed the form on page 2,
- enclosed the correct fee or an application for fee concession,
- made sufficient copies of your application and supporting documentation. You will need to submit one copy for each party to be served and one copy for the court.

Allocation questionnaire
(Small claims track)

Completed by, or on behalf of, (print name)

Reeves Publishing Ltd

who is the [Claimant][Defendant] in this claim.

Name of court	
Upton County Court	
Claim No.	2UP01222
Last date for filing with court office	xx/xx/xx

Please read the notes on pages 4 before completing the questionnaire.

You must complete **all** sections of this questionnaire. It will be used to assist the court in the management of the claim.

You should note the date by which it must be returned and the name of the court it should be returned to since this may be different from the court where proceedings were issued. This information is shown on the Form N152 which came with this questionnaire.

If you have settled this claim (or if you settle it on a future date) and therefore do not need a hearing, you must let the court know immediately.

Settlement

Would you like to use the free small claims mediation service provided by HM Courts & Tribunals Service, to help you settle your claim with the other party? ☑ Yes ☐ No

If you tick Yes, you must still complete the rest of this form.

Location of hearing

Is there any reason why the case needs to be heard at a particular court? ☐ Yes ☑ No

If Yes, say which court and why

Track

Do you agree that the small claims track is the most suitable track for this claim? ☑ Yes ☐ No

If No, please say why

D **Witnesses**

So far as you know at this stage, how many witnesses (other than yourself) do you intend to call to give evidence at the hearing? 1

E **Experts**

Do you want permission to use an expert's report at the hearing? ***(see notes)*** ☐ Yes ☑ No

If Yes, what will the expert's evidence deal with?

Have you already obtained an expert's report? ☐ Yes ☑ No

If Yes, have you given a copy of that report to the other party? ☐ Yes ☑ No

In addition to using an expert's report do you want your expert to attend the hearing and give evidence? ☐ Yes ☑ No

If Yes, give the reasons why you think their attendance is necessary:

The court may order the appointment of a single expert who can be instructed by both parties. If you think this would not be appropriate, please say why.

F **Hearing**

Are there any days within the next four months when you, an expert or a witness will not be able to attend court for the hearing? ☑ Yes ☐ No

If Yes, please give details

	Dates not available
Yourself	
Expert	
Other essential witness	21 - 25 July; 8 August - 15 August; 12 - 16 October

Will you be using an interpreter at the hearing either for yourself or for a witness? ***(see notes)*** ☐ Yes ☑ No

If Yes, please specify the type of interpreter

G Other information

In the space below, set out any other information you consider will help the judge to manage or clarify the claim, including any other information you consider should be supplied by the other party.

We estimate that the hearing will take 1 hour

H Fee

Have you attached the fee for filing this allocation questionnaire? ☑ Yes ☐ No

An allocation fee is payable if your claim or counterclaim exceeds £1,500.

Additional fees will be payable at further stages of the court process.

Signature *(see notes)*

Signed ______ Date xx/xx/xx

Print full name Brian Reeves

If a solicitor is acting for you please enter the firm's name, reference number and full postal address including (if appropriate) details of fax number, e-mail address, Document Exchange (DX) number. Otherwise, please enter your details as appropriate. This will assist the court in contacting you, if necessary at short notice.

Reeves Publishing Ltd 10 Market Place Upton UP1 1PA	Ref. no.	BR
	Telephone no.	
	Mobile no.	
	Fax no.	
	e-mail address	
	DX no.	

Notes for completing a small claims track allocation questionnaire

- If the claim is not settled, a judge must allocate it to an appropriate case management track and if necessary give directions for the conduct of the case. The most just and cost-effective track for this claim appears to be the small claims track and you must now complete the attached questionnaire to help the judge decide.
- If you fail to return the allocation questionnaire by the date given, the judge may make an order that leads to your claim or defence being 'struck out' (Civil Procedure Rules (CPR) Rule 3.4): this means you could not proceed with it. Alternatively the judge may order an allocation hearing at which the judge can order any party who has not filed their questionnaire to pay, immediately, the costs of that hearing.
- The letters below refer to the corresponding sections of the questionnaire and tell you what information is needed, including where appropriate other guidance and references to court rules.

A Settlement

Even at this stage, you should still think about whether you and the other party can settle your dispute without going to court. You may seek to settle the claim either by direct discussion or negotiation with the other party or by mediation. Mediation is a way of resolving disputes without needing to go to a court hearing, where parties are assisted in achieving mutually beneficial resolutions with the help of an impartial mediator. You may use any mediation provider, but if you would like to try the free HM Courts & Tribunals Service small claims mediation service, or find out more about how mediation could help, you should tick 'Yes' to this question. The court will then refer your case to the small claims mediator and provide you with a contact telephone number. Experience has shown that it is often possible for the mediator to help resolve disputes over the telephone without either party having to attend court. However, since mediation is a voluntary process, it will only take place if the parties agree.

Even if you tick 'Yes' in Section A, you should still complete the rest of the form before returning it to the court centre.

B Location

Automatic transfer to a more appropriate court applies to certain claims (CPR 26). This claim may be heard in a different court from which you have been asked to return the form. When transferring to a different court the court that you indicate and your reasons will be taken into consideration.

C Track

The basic guide by which claims are normally allocated to a track is the amount in dispute, although other factors such as the complexity of the case will also be considered (CPR 26). Leaflet EX306 - The Small claims track in civil courts, explains this in greater detail.

D Witnesses

Enter the number of witnesses you intend to call to give evidence **not** including yourself or any expert witness.

E Experts

You should **not** obtain an expert's report until you receive the court's direction. If you have already obtained a report, please attach it to your completed questionnaire.

F Hearing

Dates to avoid: You should only enter those dates where you, your expert or an essential witness will not be able to attend court because of a holiday or other commitments.

Interpreters: In some circumstances the court will arrange for, and meet the cost of, an interpreter. If you require an interpreter, you should contact the court immediately. For further details visit our website www.justice.gov.uk under 'guidance'.

G Other information

Give details of any other information that you consider will help the judge to manage the claim, referring as necessary to any documents you have attached. Bear in mind however that at this stage you need not attach all other documents which you wish the court to consider at the hearing. This is something you will later be asked to provide.

H Fee

For more information about court fees please go to the website hmctsformfinder.justice.gov.uk or pick up a fees leaflet EX50 from any county court. If you cannot afford the fee, you may be eligible for remission of the fee. More details can be found in the leaflet EX160A, which can be downloaded from our website or you can pick up a copy from any county court.

I Signature

This questionnaire must be signed by only the party to the claim or litigation friend or legal representative.